DATE DUE

~~MR 10 '98~~		
~~JE 13 05~~		
~~DE 18 09~~		
2-19-10		

DEMCO 38-296

Catering
Like a Pro

From Planning
to Profit

FRANCINE HALVORSEN

John Wiley & Sons, Inc.

New York • Chichester • Brisbane • Toronto • Singapore

:mories of
ıg Geffner
d
Dr. Werner Engel

This text is printed on acid-free paper.

Copyright © 1994 by Francine Halvorsen

All rights reserved. Published simultaneously in Canada.

Reproduction or translation of any part of this work beyond that permitted by Section 107 or 108 of the 1976 United States Copyright Act without the permission of the copyright owner is unlawful. Requests for permission or further information should be addressed to the Permissions Department, John Wiley & Sons, Inc.

This publication is designed to provide accurate and authoritative information in regard to the subject matter covered. It is sold with the understanding that the publisher is not engaged in rendering professional services. If legal, accounting, medical, psychological, or any other expert assistance is required, the services of a competent professional person should be sought. ADAPTED FROM A DECLARATION OF PRINCIPLES OF A JOINT COMMITTEE OF THE AMERICAN BAR ASSOCIATION AND PUBLISHERS.

Library of Congress Cataloging-in-Publication Data:

Halvorsen, Francine.
    Catering like a pro : from planning to profit / Francine Halvorsen.
        p.   cm.
    Includes bibliographical references
    ISBN 0-471-00688-2 (cloth ; acid-free paper) — ISBN 0-471-59522-5 (paper)
        1. Caterers and catering—Handbooks, manuals, etc. I. Title.
    TX721.H3   1993
    641'.4—dc20

                                                        93-29809

Printed in the United States of America

10 9 8 7 6 5 4 3

Acknowledgments

I want to thank "the pros" who give truth to the saying that if you want something done, ask a busy person. Annemarie Colbin, Ronnie Davis, Francois Dionot, Steve Frankel, Jonathan Horst, Bob Kinkead, Joe McDonnell, Jim McMullen, Jacques Pepin, Stanley Poll, Sylvia Weinstock.

Each of them works, as Joe McDonnell said, "everyday but St. Swithun's," and all hours except 2 to 5 in the morning and sometimes even then. Jan Anderson at Illycafe was generous with her time and coffee expertise.

Heide Lange at Sanford Greenburger needs to be thanked for her support and enthusiasm. I want to thank Audrey Melkin for introducing me to John Wiley and Claire Thompson for her knowledge, thoughtfulness and good humor. Jane Ward and Angela Murphy, in addition to their professional skills are exceptional telephone communicators, no small plus.

My gratitude to Irena Chalmers for her generous vote of confidence and encouragement when I needed it.

The various and extended attentions of Jesse Halvorsen and Lionel Halvorsen to my concerns in writing this book have been not only valuable, but greatly enjoyable, and I thank them.

Contents

Foreword

I have always been fascinated with small bits of information, like knowing mathematicians are often music lovers because they respond to the strong mathematicial discipline of music that goes way beyond the superficial beat of one, two, three. Lawyers and doctors have a lot in common because both require extensive deductive reasoning skills. It does not, therefore, come as a surprise to discover the new breed of food professionals are expert in both the arts and the sciences. Francine is a painter and poet. She also uses the language of food as her palette and food as her canvas. It has made her an exceptional cook.

Francine is the caterer and friend we could all wish we had in our neighborhood. She is generous in contributing her own unique style of cooking and presentation to raise funds for dozens of causes and her generosity is reflected in her dedication to make every party an event and every event a party. Always she errs on the side of bringing a little more of everything for everyone.

Francine Halvorsen has the experience and qualifications to write this book. She has staged literally hundreds of parties under all manner of abundant and circumscribed conditions. She has thrived in the rich beauty and resources of Florence and has come up with brilliant on-site solutions when faced with a scarcity of food and equipment in remote locations.

In *Catering Like a Pro* Francine Halvorsen describes in detail all the behind-the-scene techniques necessary to be a professional. Reading it is an apprenticeship in catering from start to finish. It is a book that should be kept nearby and called upon as a dependable consultant to confer with again and again.

Catering is among the most demanding areas of the food business. A caterer must be charming and inspire confidence or no client will be willing to entrust what may be the most important event of their life. They must be knowledgeable and flexible while simultaneously being an astute businessperson who remembers to carefully add up all the hidden costs so that there are no surprises either for caterer or for client. They must combine the skills of a psychiatrist, plumber, electrician, flat-tire changer and be able to cope with everything that can go wrong, from finding the furnace is on fire to calming a host or hostess in full heat. In addition, a caterer must have the skills to organize the event, plan the meal, cook the food, serve it, wash the dishes, and get the pots back to home base after a fourteen-hour day. That anyone would take this on is amazing. That anyone would be prepared to reveal how it can be done is inspiring. That Francine Halvorsen has written this book is her gift to us.

IRENA CHALMERS

New York

Preface

I hope, as with all really useful guides, this book's attention to detail will free the readers to be confident and creative as they pursue their careers. People often omit professional requirements because they seem obscure and overwhelming. The chapters will take you from first thoughts and how to clarify them, to organizing a large off-premise party, exposing and explaining the specifics.

The phrase "easier said than done" was invented for the applied arts. This book has been devised to enable someone using it to follow step-by-step all the sections that, when assembled, make for successful client-centered events.

All the practical considerations are covered, some are technical and some are common sense, from business-office management and finance, computer catering-programs to telephone hotlines for a more confident, less stressful professional life.

The professionals interviewed: Annemarie Colbin, Ronnie Davis, Francois Dionot, Steve Frankel, Jonathan Horst, Bob Kinkead, Joe McDonnell, Jim McMullen, Jacques Pepin, Stanley Poll, Sylvia Weinstock are each worth listening to. Their combined expertise is awesome and they have unselfishly shared their experience.

Coming together at a catered occasion is a social event first and an eating event second. That being said, the food should be excellent. The menus in the book can be used as they are or to give you ideas that you adapt to suit your needs. All the recipes are for 20 or more and most of them can be halved or doubled. Most regional markets have all the food you will need, but the copious directories will provide endless food resources and a lifeline to large-scale recipes that suit any tastes.

Given the varieties of conditions and circumstances in which a caterer has to create memorable food, heeding the basics is everything. If you are uninformed about food storage and sanitation, goodwill and good humor will be short lived. And clearly your delicious food is useless if there are not enough place settings or the service staff is late and grumpy. The checklists and charts will help you keep track of everything you need.

The names, addresses, and phone numbers in the directories will enable you access to your own independent network, and build up pesonal data files. This book is not meant to be read and discarded but kept on hand as a reference book. Amateurs and professionals alike will find particular ways to bring order and organization to ideas and execute them as they are needed. As you learn each element you are encouraged to build on what you know.

Catering is a profession that evolves with perseverance and though it requires substantial skill, in the long run it is the personal and necessary intangibles that you bring to catering—your signature touches and the interpersonal relationship you develop with colleagues and clients—that will build your reputation.

FRANCINE HALVORSEN

ONE

The Client-Centered Approach to Catering

Catering is a perfect business for goal-oriented people who find problem solving a challenging and pleasurable game. It's sometimes like being the ringmaster of a traveling circus, guiding performers and guests through a series of events, which appear to be wonderfully spontaneous, but are the result of dozens of quite practical decisions.

If you are like most people who think about doing professional catering, you love food, parties, and people. When your family and friends ask you to take charge of events at holidays and personal celebrations you say yes almost every time. You enjoy making special occasions memorable and prefer the hard work and rewards of these endeavors to whatever else you are already doing. Developing an equal enthusiasm for learning, planning, organizing, and earning more money than you spend on any event will transform you from an amateur to a professional caterer. Add the stamina to deliver the event, and you are a thriving entrepreneur.

Off-premise catering requires personality traits that at first seem contradictory. While catering is appealing to many free spirits, it demands a great deal of organization and administration to channel bursts of inspiration and creative impulses. Everything must be planned to the last detail, yet carried out with extreme flexibility, to allow the caterer to respond to the wishes of clients, technical difficulties, people problems, and the vicissitudes of weather. Many

1

people feel that stamina and a smile are more important than culinary skills, but your clients will expect both from you.

No single formula can be carved in stone, and that's why experienced professionals report the need to have dependable client-interview techniques, good management ability, reliable help, creative food planning, product resources, and the vitality and clearheadedness to stay on top of each job thoroughly from start to finish. Your main bankable assets are the interpersonal and negotiating abilities that will help you prosper.

Organizing procedures and estimating costs maximize results and minimize losses. By and large, catering earns a greater profit margin than the restaurant business, but there is not much room for error as the food profit markup is not very great. Even the most luxurious of foods and feasts must be analyzed economically. The expensive treats and labor intensive goodies that bring oohs and ahs from your friends and family will be few and far between since most of your clients will not give you a blank check.

By far the largest number of new entrants to this business do off-premise catering, which usually means having a professional kitchen and office but no fixed banquet hall or dining area. Selling even small amounts of food from your kitchen may be a legal gray area in some communities, and you need to check local health department codes. Look for a properly licensed kitchen you can use if you are starting out with minimum capital. Often small restaurants, specialty food shops, private schools, and religious or community centers will rent space and time in their kitchens during their off-hours or lulls. This is another area where networking helps, so ask around.

Schools, religious organizations, businesses, political groups, civic associations, and fund-raisers are held accountable in planning their regular and special occasion events. People arranging private family celebrations have limited assets, whatever their bank account. Clearly, money managing will be one of your important tasks.

Another valuable grace is flexibility. You have to be in charge of all levels of each project, each has to reflect your tastes and standards. Yet, you cannot be overly controlling because it is your client's wishes that must be satisfied and your colleagues' cooperation that you depend on. People call caterers to execute projects that are important to them and they want the result to be something more than good food. They want a memorable event that makes them feel it was something they would have done if only they could. You may be surprised at the details they feel passionately about. As your reputation increases, people will listen to you more, but your first job is to listen to the client.

What makes catering different from other professional culinary fields is that each and every job is unique and must be planned from beginning to end to satisfy the demands of the client.

You will need to keep a pencil handy so you can make notes, organize them, and read back to your client what it is they want. Then it must be translated into an achievable plan. Your clients will vary from knowing exactly what they want, without a clue as to what it takes to achieve it, to the people who just want to select from clear-cut options you have to offer. The same questions must be asked and answered repeatedly: How many? How much? Where? When? What? Why? Who? All professionals report the same two things: "You must write everything down" and "There's always something." Caterers are often independent risk takers, but they must also be team players; excellent organizers, but not control freaks. Be prepared to deliver exactly on schedule and equally prepared to wait for a late guest of honor, traffic jams, power outages, or security checks.

When you are starting out, it is ounce wise and pound foolish to scrimp on the time and money it takes to research and develop your confidence and techniques. Dry runs for family and friends or charity events, for which only the materials are paid for, are an investment of your time that will pay off in the future.

Professionals readily acknowledge that it takes special skills and planning to make delicious and attractive food off-premises that is just right for each circumstance. They do not function from inspiration to inspiration, rather, they count on dependable methods and recipes to turn out a professional product at a profit. They know people are depending on them, and that expensive experiments are rarely fun and could be embarrassments. Under a wide range of conditions, caterers must be able to provide food that looks as appetizing as it tastes delicious, and make money doing it. Not one caterer calls it an easy job.

Besides a personal style, this business demands that you keep current with trends in food fashions and entertaining styles. The pros all read trade journals, magazines, and the food section of major newspapers as well as many of the food industry newsletters. This is something you can start doing now.

The dictionary defines "caterer" as "One who supplies the viands at an entertainment," "Cate (s)—provisions bought . . . usually considered to be more delicate or dainty than home production." "Acate—provisions not made in the house, but purchased fresh when wanted." "Acater—a purchaser of provisions, purveyor; provider, or preparer of eats or delicacies; a cater or caterer." As early as the fifteenth century, "to cate" was a profession, but every caterer interviewed here repeated, "Cooking is the least of it."

Local markets vary in what they have to offer and the seasons bring different foods to market; substituting ingredients in recipes or menus may be necessary. Caterers have to bear in mind incremental cost ratios of proportions for ten, twenty-five, and fifty people, and the proportional preparation and cooking times. The most experienced chefs can sometimes omit a step from their checklist if they are not mindful. Professionals have to be informed on capital and overhead costs and how to analyze and predict job expenses.

If you are going to provide provisions only—with no, or virtually no services—consider what corner of the culinary market you want to claim. Visualize what it is you want to do. Be as specific as possible. Think of the food and services you want to provide and of your abilities and your resources. The more explicit you are about what you do and do not provide, the happier everyone will be.

Do you want to make food à la carte? Cook to order and deliver, or have it picked up? There is potential for any single product to meet with success; people have built happy lives on muffins, cakes, sushi, chili, pasta, soups, and so on.

Is your specialty: birthday parties; holiday themes; office lunches; beach parties; elegant dining; cakes and pastries? Do you feel more comfortable with buffet meals and informal settings for large groups, or do you shine when you assemble dinner from scratch for twenty people?

Families growing weary of the sameness of fast-food deliveries are calling on chefs to deliver a home-cooked meal to them when they return from work.

Begin a personal directory of resources and potential clients that includes people you know who use caterers and people who have asked you to cook special dishes or to plan events and special celebrations. Start to keep a small set of file folders for your notes and the information you glean from newspapers, magazines, and other resources. Sometimes information crosses your path when you are in a hurry, and if you are organized you can review it at your convenience.

Since many caterers start by simply making and delivering food to order, organize your recipe files and menus. They are good merchandising tools and helpful in systematizing food and nonfood items.

Students in the field of hotel and restaurant management are often comfortable and capable with food but need to find out the seemingly hidden elements that make a catered event work. Whether you are starting a full-service catering establishment or specializing in a small corner of the market, you need all the practice you can get.

The best way to begin finding clients is by word of mouth. Once you let it be known that you are willing to provide a catering service, family and friends will be your first network. Every organization or group with which you are associated can be told you are available for catering events. Read not only the major newspapers but the local and neighborhood papers that carry news of upcoming events, new buildings opening, new companies or functions coming to town. Check the library for magazines and books. The yellow pages are another excellent resource. Don't be reluctant to call organizations you would like as clients. Find out who is in charge of contracting caterers and either speak to them or mail them an introductory letter and follow up by phone.

Speak with people who are frequently asked if they know a good caterer, such as neighborhood merchants who specialize in gourmet food and kitchen supplies, bridal consultants and bridal clothiers, florists, and even bookstores.

Find out who handles local government events like Fourth of July celebrations, inaugurations, and landmark anniversaries; see if you can work with them in some capacity. Have business cards and letterheads printed so that you have a professional demeanor from the start. Treat the people you talk with as potential contacts or clients.

Catering is a versatile and fast growing segment of the flourishing foodservice industry. Do not turn your nose up at any assignment you think you can handle, think of it as being paid to build experience and a resume.

COLLONGES, le 26 Août

Madame F. HALVORSEN

Chère Madame,

                    voici ce que je pense de la
cuisine de catering:

"Il y a une réelle évolution ces dernières
années, les prestations servies sur l'ensemble
des compagnies sont supérieures.

Le seul conseil que je puisse donner c'est de
réaliser des plats simples avec des produits de
qualité.

Et, chose très importante, il faut que
l'équipage ait le souire!"

Bien amicalement.

Defining and Achieving Your Goals

How do your family and friends feel about what you are doing? Are they supportive? Catering requires a lot of long hours and intense concentration that cannot be postponed. Deadlines have to be honored and they are usually on weekends and holidays.

Working for a caterer or even volunteering for some special events will provide the experience of on-the-job pressures that occur. It will also be an opportunity to see firsthand the unplanned glitches that must be dealt with.

What goals do you have for the next three to five years? What are your financial requirements and how are you going to fulfill them? Will you use your savings or borrow? Will you keep the job you have and work in the food profession early mornings or at night? Will you cater on weekends? Are you going to jump into it full time? Try to write down your thoughts and turn them into a strategy.

A great deal of free information is available from public libraries, various government offices, and schools. The Small Business Administration, the United States Government Printing Office, and the National Restaurant Association all have a miscellany of helpful information, as do the culinary schools in your area.

The first rush of business from family, friends, neighbors, and colleagues will probably be the cornerstone you build on. Plan things out thoroughly, deliver a little more than what you promise, and the favorable impression you make on the guests at these events can increase your business exponentially. When contacted by potential clients who have been to one of your previous events, present food and ambience not too different from the flavors and functions that led them to choose you in the first place.

Listen to people at events you orchestrate. They are quick to tell you the best and the worst. Adjust and respond; perhaps less has to be spent on food and more on service, or the decor was too elaborate, and there wasn't a generous amount of glassware. You want it not just to work but to appear perfect.

Each client has a certain style of event that is the most comfortable for them. Often cultural or corporate clients favor caterers that understand their goals. Thoughtful letters and menus, occasional tasting parties, or sample gift baskets remind people of what you are good at.

If you are already working at a full-time job, you might want to make yourself available to work for a caterer or other food service on weekends and see how an event goes from beginning to end. Nothing you learn is wasted. No matter how well staffed you plan to be, sooner or later you will have to do every aspect of catering. Due to unforeseeable emergencies you may find yourself scraping dishes and repacking them, after scouting the premises with a flashlight for dropped flatware. But if you are doing it when the "emergency" was foreseeable, you haven't planned well. Pacing yourself and hiring staff are things that must be done from the beginning.

EDUCATION

Education is essential. Even if you are an excellent cook and manager, you do not want to reinvent the wheel. Preparing meals for large numbers under various conditions, and serving it graciously at the appropriate temperature and time, takes many small steps in reasonable order. Apprenticing will give you a good feel for the pace and taking a few courses in a culinary school will introduce you to methods and systems that are invaluable.

Entering an associates program, particularly if you have had little or no college, teaches many things. Not just specific skills, but how to be professional. Almost all culinary schools and college departments have excellent individual courses if you do not want to enter a long-term program. From six months to two years in a school situation and apprenticing in different capacities are a good combination. You may decide to wing it and start with only your own track record to take on professional jobs you know you can handle and learn added skills as you need them. Many professionals have started this way.

Good culinary schools offer everything from the expected courses in food, pastry, nutrition, and sanitation to the often overlooked but much needed courses in the psychology of human relations, practical accounting, and law. Schools also present the benefits of professional networking and full- or part-time job opportunities that help build your resume while you learn to run your own business. Many of them have first-rate restaurants where diners expect the best in food and service. Education credits and a good resume will also help with finances later on. Purposefulness always adds to credibility. Banks or family members will need some reassurance that you take your career seriously before they invest their money.

The schools offer updated brochures. Call the schools and ask questions or visit them and see how you can best benefit from their program.

Other resource centers for written material include the culinary collections at your public library and local colleges. For instance, Radcliffe has a collection of almost ten thousand volumes in their culinary collection in the Schlesinger Library (founded by the grandparents of Chris Schlesinger, chef and restaurateur). The library runs a series of free seminars that are open to the public. "First Mondays" meet at the library from 10 A.M. to 12 noon on the first Monday of each month on the campus in Cambridge, Massachusetts.

Chef Louis Szathmary owned the world famous Bakery restaurant in Chicago and was an avid collector of culinary literature in many languages. They include eight thousand books, thirty-five hundred pamphlets, and one hundred unpublished manuscripts. They span five hundred years, the earliest volume being from 1299. The Collection of Culinary Arts was willed by him to the University of Iowa, where he knew they would be cared for, conserved, and bound. The collection can be used to research historic meals and dinners from various periods and cultures as well as culinary history and modern recipes.

LOCATION

As you develop your business plan, looking for a location for your operation is important. When you are considering a place to run your business, zoning is a legal issue that will affect your decision. The space must be adequate for work, storage, parking, and delivery facilities. It is a good idea to make sure you will not be disturbing people when you and your crew come back, unload, and unpack at one or two in the morning.

At this point too, you will have to decide if you want to arrange things so that clients can come to you and see your kitchen and have a sampling, or go to their home or office. If clients are going to visit your premises for tastings and meetings, clearly your work space must look as good as your food tastes. For the purpose of maximizing how your space looks, you are well advised to consult with a designer.

The location caterers function from is traditionally called the commissary, which is not only a kitchen, but where provisions and staples are received, sorted, and stored, and where food is prepared and kept hot, cold, or frozen until ready to use. You need room to pack food and equipment and a place where staff can keep personal things, change, and eat. It must have a completely enclosed toilet and washroom. When you are starting, your office will probably be a corner of the commissary as well. Fire and sanitary codes must be adhered to very stringently.

To calculate the square feet you need, take an educated guess as to the size your average event will be. If you think a dinner party for one hundred will be the largest group to whom you might deliver a full meal, you will be able to plan accordingly. The same facilities will then easily accommodate a cocktail party for 250, or three simultaneous weekend parties of twenty or twenty-five each.

EQUIPMENT

You might want to consult a kitchen planner, though if you are starting small it is probably better to spend the money on the equipment itself. Places that sell professional equipment usually have experts who will be very specific about what each item can and cannot do, and what is needed for its safe installation and operation. The legal codes and standards for wiring, plumbing, ventilation, and sanitation have to be adhered to in order to have premises licensed.

Beginning businesses, ranging from partial to full service, usually begin by renting things like dishes, glasses, flatware, linens, uniforms, tables and chairs, as well as insulated containers and cabinets to store and transport by hand or with rolling dollies. There are many equipment rental services. Visit them, ask questions, read their catalogs, and make lists of what you might need for a party of twenty-five for dinner or fifty for cocktails. Add up the expenses. Do the same with florists and food distributors. This not only teaches about prices, but gives you a realistic view of what is available when you want to put together a team.

As in all endeavors, there is no one single thing that is sufficient, but it is a combination of experience, formal education, independent research, and trial and error that will get you where you're going.

SCHOOL DIRECTORY

American Institute of Baking
1213 Bakers Way
Manhattan, KS 66502
Phone: (800) 633-5137; (913) 537-4750 /
Fax: (913) 537-1493

Baltimore International Culinary College
25 South Calvert Street
Baltimore, MD 21202
Phone: (410) 752-5031 / Fax: (410) 752-4395

Bellingham Technical College
3028 Lindberg Avenue
Bellingham, WA 98225
Phone: (206) 676-6490

California Culinary Academy
625 Polk Street
San Francisco, CA 94102
Phone: (800) 229-2433; (415) 771-3536

Cambridge School of Culinary Arts
2020 Massachusetts Avenue
Cambridge, MA 01240
Phone: (617) 354-3836

Chocolate Gallery
School of Confectionery
34 West 22 Street
New York, NY 10011
Phone: (212) 675-2253

Cornell University
School of Hotel Administration
Statler Hall
Ithaca, NY 14853
Phone: (607) 256-5106

Culinary Arts Division
New School for Social Research
100 Greenwich Avenue
New York, NY 10011
Phone: (212) 255-4141

Culinary Institute of America
433 Albany Post Road
Hyde Park, NY 12538-1499
Phone: (800) 283-2433

French Culinary Institute
Jacques Pepin, Dean of Studies
Alain Sailhac, Dean of Culinary Arts
462 Broadway
New York, NY 10013
Phone: (212) 219-8890

Harriet's Kitchen
Whole Foods Cooking School
P.O. Box 1301
Winter Park, FL 32790-1301
Phone: (407) 644-2167

IACP International Directory of Cooking Schools
304 West Liberty Street, Suite 201
Louisville, KY 40202
Phone: (502) 581-9786 / Fax: (502) 589-3602

International Caterers Association
220 South State Street, Suite 1416
Chicago, IL 60604
Phone: (312) 922-1271

Johnson & Wales University
8 Abbott Park Place
Providence, RI 02903
Phone: (800) 343-2565; (401) 456-1000 /
Fax: (401) 421-9598

L'Academie de Cuisine
  Francois Dionot, President
  5021 Wilson Lane
  Bethesda, MD 20814
  Phone: (800) 445-1959; (301) 986-9490

Le Chef
  College of Hospitality Careers
  6020 Dillard Circle
  Austin, TX 78752
  Phone: (512) 323-2511

National Restaurant Association
  The Educational Foundation
  250 South Wacker Drive, Suite 1400
  Chicago, IL 60606
  Phone: (800) 765-2122

Natural Gourmet Cookery School
  48 West 21 Street, 2nd floor
  New York, NY 10011
  Phone: (212) 645-5170

New York Restaurant School
  27 West 34 Street
  New York, NY 10001
  Phone: (212) 947-7097

Peter Kump's School of Culinary Arts
  307 East 92 Street
  New York, NY 10128
  Phone: (800) 522-4610; (212) 410-5152 /
    Fax: (212) 348-6360

Radcliffe College
  The Arthur and Elizabeth Schlesinger Library
  3 James Street
  Cambridge, MA 02138
  Phone: (617) 495-8647

Santa Fe School of Cooking
116 West San Francisco Street
Santa Fe, NM 87501
Phone: (505) 983-4511 / Fax: (505) 983-7540

The Restaurant School
2129 Walnut Street
Philadelphia, PA 19103
Phone: (215) 561-3446

University of Iowa
Chef Louis Szathmary Collection of Culinary Arts
Iowa City, IA 52242
Phone: (319) 335-5921

School of Natural Cookery
P.O. Box 19466
Boulder, CO 80308-2466
Phone: (303) 444-8068

FOODSERVICE RESOURCES

International Association of Culinary Professionals
304 West Liberty Street, Suite 201
Louisville, KY 40202
Phone: (502) 581-9786

International Association of Women Chefs and Restaurateurs
401 East 80 Street, Suite 4K
New York, NY 10021
Phone: (212) 879-2709 / Fax: (212) 861-1367

International Special Events Society
P.O. Box 6625, Yorkville Station
New York, NY 10128
Phone: (212) 876-3500 / Fax: (212) 996-4815
(Local chapters in cities throughout the country)

National Association of Catering Executives
304 West Liberty Street, Suite 201
Louisville, KY 40202
Phone: (502) 583-3783 / Fax: (502) 589-3602

Roundtable for Women in Foodservice
205 East 78 Street, Suite 1A
New York, NY 10021
Phone: (212) 439-0580 / Fax: (212) 688-6457
(Local chapters in cities throughout the country)

Small Business Administration
Answer Desk
Phone: (800) U-ASK-SBA

United States Government Printing Office
Superintendent of Documents
710 Capitol Street, N.W.
Washington, DC 20401
Phone: (202) 783-3238 / Fax: (202) 512-2250

THREE

Talking with the Professionals

RONNIE DAVIS, WASHINGTON STREET CAFE, NEW YORK

Ronnie Davis, who is the CEO of Washington Street Cafe, has a well deserved reputation as a major problem solver. "Be dressed" means one thing—a tuxedo, wing-collar shirt, and black dress socks and shoes. Yes, that's for men *and* women. The business uses as many as three hundred waitpersons a week in addition to a permanent staff of thirty-five.

Davis's grandfather, father, and uncle were caterers in Philadelphia and he has known his way around a professional kitchen since he was five years old. He peeled potatoes and boiled eggs, bused tables, was a waiter, and, at 16 a headwaiter. He learned his skills with a group of multiracial waiters in Philadelphia that traveled to hotels, celebrations, and Pullman dining cars. Davis says he learned that service is an art with great dignity. And because his father owned the business he wanted to gain everyone's respect. He also earned a lot of his own money as a waiter by doing five parties a weekend when he was in school. At 18 he became a banquet manager for the Hilton. He then apprenticed with a fine chef.

He himself was the chef when he opened the Washington Street Cafe in 1980 and for several years he ran it as a restaurant and catering business. His catering reputation got "too good too fast" and it was clear, that was his special talent. He kept the name because he preferred to have a corporate entity, so that clients would understand that his staff reflected the cafe's standards as well as he. Everyone thinks "Their caterer" is the best. "My mother makes the best soup. My mother makes the best meat loaf, pie, et cetera."

His enormous ability to take situations that are potentially difficult and attack them logistically has brought him stellar clients from all areas, from the Grammy Awards and Lincoln Center dinners for 450, to big political parties for three thousand, from fund-raising events that are hard to say no to, to corporate and private clients who celebrate special occasions. A food perfectionist, Davis has the head chef and kitchen staff bring everything for him to taste as it will actually be presented to the client. For parties over two hundred, the client will get to have a tasting sampler.

People call about events two years in advance as well as for next month. Davis thinks an experienced party planner can design any event within ten hours. While more lead time is beneficial, two to three weeks is ample to organize most functions. Everyone on the staff has to have explicit assignments.

"You have to ask yourself what your strength is and work from there. Learn what you don't know, even if you wind up hiring others to do it. Learn the back of the house, bus, wash dishes, see what happens to five hundred dirty place settings, track the sanitation, and clean up. Learn bartending—how to deal with liquor for five hundred, what is possible, how people react to different kinds of service and presentation.

"Learn about buying, checking orders, loading the food, getting the food to the location. How do you pack? How will it be transported? Will you be able to use a handcart, or do you have to carry it? Be a sous chef. What does a head chef do at a party? Who administers it, sets it up, cleans up?"

Davis uses a function sheet, which is on his personalized computer. The program has letters and contracts, but the function sheet is the one that lists the date of intake, name of client and who booked the job, where it is to be held, the nature of the event, administrative needs, licenses for liquor, parking, fireworks, using a public place. What kitchen staff will be needed, where do they leave from and when?

"Ask the driver if more than one is necessary. Will they encounter a situation where a second driver has to park the van or take it to another location, while the first delivers and maybe unpacks? What is the condition of the vehicle? What equipment is needed on the van? Is anyone meeting them at the site?

"When interviewing potential clients, one must listen to what they want and not judge. The job of the caterer is to professionally make people happy. It is your charter to interpret what the client wants and extrapolate the specifics that let you deliver. You have to patiently show them how you can make what they want happen. Budget is another thing. Some clients have no idea how expensive each additional item or station can be. Not merely the ingredients but the preparation, the serving, and the cleanup. You will be well compensated, but you cannot dictate your taste or be all things to all people.

"You have an obligation to explain why you can't do something your client wants if you know it can't be done or that it is something you won't do. If your client still wants it, recommend they see someone else."

JACQUES PEPIN, FRENCH CULINARY INSTITUTE, NEW YORK

L'École is the restaurant of the French Culinary Institute in New York's Soho, a block away from the newly renovated cast-iron landmark that houses the downtown Guggenheim Museum. Jacques Pepin is the Dean of Studies.

A calmer, more gracious host cannot be imagined. His schedule includes not only courses at FCI and Boston University, but television and lecture appearances, writing, consulting, and creating culinary legends. His advice for beginning caterers—simplicity.

"A salad composé. Wash and drain the salad, marinate the

chicken, prepare the mushrooms and fresh garnish. Prepare and wrap the salad; prepare the dressing and store it separately. On the premises, sauté or grill chicken breasts and mushrooms, top with your choice of something fresh, and then prepare the plates individually and serve fifty easily. If asked to entertain fifteen hundred, I would say, yes of course, and then buy the best bread, the best prosciutto, the best of cheese and fruit; I do not really attempt to cook for that many if I am alone. I shop and prepare and present. For five hundred, perhaps, I poach several salmon and dress them cold for a buffet. If I am a beginner, perhaps for ten to twenty, every last bit is from scratch.

"The selection of materials is very important, choose selectively. Break the menu down in your head. The size of the kitchen and the equipment is critical. Inspect the site and if you cannot do that, don't assume anything. You cannot duplicate exactly a previous situation.

"To develop, you have to understand a recipe. You start with an idea to make A and B and then when you have created an entity you respond to the food as it takes shape. When you become so familiar with it that you have it in depth, you adjust to the feel of it. You know it so well, you can do *this* and not do *that* and finish it with the proper result for two hundred. You will know it well enough to adjust for moisture, for dryness, for an oven too hot, or a dinner too late. The base product will feel right to you and you will be able to finish it with the proper results in a variety of conditions. Catering is not a question of self-consciously expressing yourself. Your craftsmanship will do that."

SYLVIA WEINSTOCK, SYLVIA WEINSTOCK'S CAKES, NEW YORK

In Sylvia Weinstock's sunny Tribeca location, the phone never stops ringing. Without missing a beat, she takes each call with genuine interest and enthusiasm, pausing only momentarily to confirm dates and times in a leather agenda. It is no wonder that many of her colleagues and clients have become friends.

Always a successful home baker, when an illness kept her housebound she started making more elaborate cakes as a creative hobby, producing more than friends and family could devour. She took these to local restaurants who bought as many as she could deliver. They started placing orders and by the time she was better, she was in business. Keeping her cake recipes simple and dependable, Sylvia Weinstock has brought the art of sugar decorating and sculpting to new heights.

After delivering a birthday cake a friend had ordered for a party at an elegant New York hotel, she called the banquet manager to see how he liked it. Impressed by both the cake and her professionalism, he ordered a cake for a wedding and the rest is cake history.

She creates cakes for private and public events, museum and corporate affairs, and social and celebrity galas. Clients have been known to fly her and her cakes wherever their party is. Though many clients are celebrities, she says all her clients are special and the cakes she delivers attest to that philosophy. She developed a special sugar blend that can be made into flowers and other forms ahead of time. It can be manipulated by hand so that botanically correct flowers or fanciful ornamentation are stunning when made by skilled artisans. It sometimes takes two weeks to make the decoration for one cake. People not only eat the decorations but take some home as souvenirs.

"Still the most important part of the job is the interview, finding out what people's expectations are and translating them into what is doable. The cakes are, after all, for dream occasions and people want nothing less than their dream satisfied. The purpose is to please the client, to deliver what they want. The next is the follow up. Call the banquet manager or the client. Ask. Did you like it? I really wait for that 'Yes.' It is important to me."

She doesn't advertise but lets her unique custom cakes, commitment, responsibility, long hours, and creativity speak for themselves.

About specializing. "We don't want to do it all. Our cakes are so labor intensive, that even with special skills it would be hard to perfect them and pay attention to delivering an equally good meal."

Sylvia Weinstock says it is important for people starting out to know that they will have to put the business first seven days a week, that it is service that is being sought and paid for. And, yes, a certain amount of tension and anxiety are a normal part of operating successfully.

JIM MCMULLEN, JIM MCMULLEN'S RESTAURANT AND CATERING, NEW YORK

For restaurateurs who are thinking about the catering business, Jim McMullen is an exception that proves the rule. A successful model in New York, he decided to open a restaurant on the Upper East Side of Manhattan in 1975 with $20,000 and no experience. Two years later he moved around the corner to his present location, where he has been in business for almost twenty years.

McMullen wanted to go into a business and says he chose the restaurant business somewhat arbitrarily only because he knew people in the field. He had never before worked in a restaurant and was barely familiar with what the back of the house looked like. "I was a yo-yo. A fortunate yo-yo." One with uncommon common sense, too. He says that he started with simple food, like hamburgers, and chicken potpies. "People's palates weren't sophisticated then. Now, dozens of cuisines later, everyone is back to comfort food. People started wanting private parties and since I had a large kitchen and a dining room I could close off I was soon catering on premises regularly. As requests grew I bought a building down the block in which I opened a large off-premise kitchen devoted to catering. There is a banquet manager, catering chef, and staff. The wait staff are usually people who have worked in the restaurant, so there is a relaxed spirit."

McMullen contrasts the fixed menu of the restaurant with what he thinks of as the almost unlimited possibilities of catering. "Equipment is extremely important. For parties in the neighborhood, food can virtually go from oven to event. For events further afield the service staff must be equipped to cook off-premise at any function. Most restaurants are asked to cater. And restaurateurs must ask themselves if they have a large enough kitchen and storage space to do catering without closing their restaurant. What can they deliver that will please a client that may be expecting the same things they have eaten in the restaurant? Kitchens are getting smaller and smaller as rents get higher and each square foot has to produce income. A restaurateur might consider renting another kitchen or even a clean storage space where off-premise equipment can be stored. It is easy to lose money catering, as it is very labor intensive in different ways than the restaurant business, and you can't go to the client a few days before their event and tell them double the price. You have to have an organized mind. I catered my own wedding for six hundred people under a tent on Sutton Place.

"It's not about being creative, it's about organization. Thinking about diverse things at the same time—can the glasses be washed and reused or do you have to have an enormous amount? Do the waiters have their own gloves? How will everything be transported? When, and in what order? It takes serious management skills. Everything has to work. It's a second cousin to the restaurant business, not immediate family. Also, because it's a special event, people want everything in its place. That's what they remember. They are not as forgiving as they are in a restaurant. I was lucky, but I would advise someone getting started to get a job as a waiter with a substantial caterer and see how it works. If they can, they should work in the kitchen. Be prepared for a long haul getting steady work.

"Getting started is a long selling job and you have to be out there working at getting clients. Publicists are expensive and never guarantee results. Someone might want to consider going into partnership with one and see how it works if there is a vested interest in the business. Going to conventions and networking hasn't been the way for me. I didn't find people too eager to share. That's changing now—getting better—but early on when I started it was not as open.

"I always knew I wanted to run a place that other people wanted to eat at. If that coincided with my taste, fine, but the moment you cease to be objective you lose something. I have been through various cuisines as people wanted to try different things but I always kept old standards on the menu. I like taking a somewhat traditional, moderate tack that has a broad base, even though people are more sophisticated than when I started. I prefer to cater that way too. I do some really large parties but I prefer a group of up to four hundred, because each service can get more attention.

"The catering business can lose money. You can really get your head handed to you if you don't figure it all out ahead of time. You can't tell the client you didn't cover your expenses—they'll laugh you to court. The main reason for success is the ability to grow and develop. Evolve a concept, but be there to please. There are food swings, but the base remains the same."

Jonathan Horst, Adobo Catering, Santa Fe

You can't really serve caviar in Santa Fe. Even on ice, it dehydrates quickly in the ninety-five-degree dry heat. Jonathan Horst, who recently became the owner of Adobo Catering in Santa Fe, has developed a contemporary Southwest cuisine that is a blend of the best of Central and South America, Native American with a touch of California and Texas. It's a lot more than corn, squash, and beans. At a recent celebrity dinner for sixty-five not only were the guests raving about the enchiladas, rice, and beans but the tortilla soup, which features crisp tortillas in a broth of chicken stock, tomato, onion, garlic, cilantro, and epizote, blended with heavy cream.

Unfortunately the flan collapsed on the long rocky road to the party, so the guests had to make do with fresh coconut ice cream. Adobo does a lot of work for art galleries, cultural centers, and private parties in the homes and second homes of people from all fields who have a special feeling for Santa Fe, its history and landscape. One of the most interesting locations is an old abandoned turquoise mine. The hot dry air means inventive menu planning—soups and terrines, grilled fish or fowl.

Horst comes to catering with an impressive background. Starting in New York, he worked in various capacities for more than ten years, including at Dean and DeLuca and the kitchen of Chanterelle for a year and a half, leaving to work for Susan Holland, a caterer in New York, when he realized his enthusiasm was in catering. He decided to move to Santa Fe and immediately got a job at Adobo. When the owners decided to open a couple of restaurants, he bought the business with Peter Dent, who had been a colleague at Dean and DeLuca and had his own food business in New York. For Horst the excitement of planning each function and seeing it through to a successful event is doubled because of the beauty he finds in his surroundings.

JOE MCDONNAL, MARKET PLACE CATERERS, SEATTLE

Joe McDonnal's energy and good nature are apparent as he talks about his Market Place Caterers in Seattle. He first worked as a florist and floral designer, which meant decorating for parties where he got to see the creative work going on in the kitchen. The more he did flowers, the more interested he became in food and cooking. Living in New York at that time, McDonnal started taking the Thursday evening classes offered by James Beard, Dione Lucas, and other famous cooks who shared their skills in a hands-on learning situation with small groups. His next step was Italy, where he was a chef in a restaurant outside Florence for a while, then back to New York and to Spain for a "brief trip" that lasted nine years. He opened a restaurant in Spain where time flew and then he says, "It was the classic seven-year thing, seven years and one day. I was not just homesick, but all that sun was too much, and all that noise." The perfect antidote was the beautiful Northwest where he went to visit his mother. After spending some time with an uncle, also a fabulous chef, he decided to stay.

McDonnal opened a small catering business because he thought it would be more fun than a restaurant. He was right. "It's not the same room, the same china, the same menu all the time. Catering offers a wonderful challenge and variety, in a loft, under a chestnut tree, and in the wonderful private houses and gardens of Seattle and its environs. When you work for a celebration you bring the romance back to eating. You don't get to do that in a restaurant, where things have to be more controlled and people are counting calories. People are starting to be afraid of the contents of the food they eat. Awareness is one thing, but *fear*?

"When a client contacts me, we talk, then I say I'm interested and they say they're interested. I listen really carefully because I know I have to make it logistically workable. We get off the phone and I use my design imagination. I visualize a floor plan, the decoration, sometimes even the entertainment. Often the menu is the last thing. Then I call the client and say, 'Yes, I can do it. It will cost about x number of dollars.' They take a deep breath and say yes or no, thank you. We meet and finalize the details. It should go smoothly and not take too long, but if the client takes six hours to select linens, it is your duty to spend the six hours pleasantly. From start to finish you are building a future memory and the dinner is only part of it. From first take to getting the bill, the client should be so thrilled with what you do that they are happy to pay the bill. Making people happy is a personally rewarding way to spend my time. I have stacks of mail. It's wonderful. I like it all.

"Seattle is very beautiful and filled with gorgeous gardens. Some are modest gardens that become very exciting in the summer. We do a lot of dinner dances, which are sometimes sumptuous, and private parties where people like to dress up and enjoy a casual elegance that is never conspicuous. Everyone remembers a party a few years ago for twenty-four people in someone's home. One room was set up as a small theater with a Steinway piano, and when people were seated, Ella Fitzgerald walked in. That's a memory."

Market Place Catering works with a special assistant in the kitchen, which has a staff that seems to stay and work as a team.

"The people in the office are equally important. Everything comes to a screeching halt if the wheels on this track are not in first-rate condition. Bills have to be paid and submitted in good order. You need service people who know your style and understand how you want the event to function. They are your real public relations division. From the minute clients get to the door, everything that happens and everyone they speak with is part of a special occasion. We have two vans and do menus that can be delivered hot or cold from our kitchen, or prepared off-premise. So much depends on what you can do at the last minute. It is physically hard work. There is no separate moving company, no separate sanitation crew. A lot of the work is as unglamorous as you can get. The hours are hell. Eighteen-hour days are not unusual when you are busy. And you have to take the work when it is there and deliver without compromising quality. Forget holidays, except for maybe St. Swithun's Day—you're working. Forget dinner with family and friends—you are busy until one in the morning, working while others play. It's quite a rush and sometimes your alternatives for recreation are very limited and companionship restricted. You really have to figure out how to deal with the stress of work and how to make time for family and friends."

STEVE FRANKEL, NOSMOKING, NEW YORK

After he left college, Steve Frankel knew he didn't want to go to graduate school or a long-term culinary institute. He went to the New York Restaurant School, which had its own restaurant and offered an eighteen-week course. "During the first twelve weeks the mornings were spent learning basic techniques, handling different knives, and butchering and preparing fish, seafood, meat, and poultry. In the afternoon there was classroom work in various business skills, including management, cost control, sanitation, and nutrition. The last six weeks were spent working in the restaurant and preparing a proposal for a restaurant. The school offered basic concepts and skills, so that you wouldn't embarrass yourself when you went out to find an entry-level job.

"I got a job cooking in a not very good restaurant that is now closed. I learned quickly how *not* to do things. They were very disorganized and didn't treat the staff well at all. The management was out of town a lot and then spread the blame when they came back. I knew I wanted a place where people wanted to work and stay because they liked it. People who work with me know pretty quickly if they are going to like it or not. If they leave, they leave almost immediately, and the ones who stay, stay a long time."

Steve Frankel opened Exterminator Chili in Tribeca in the early eighties and it was a very large success for several years until he decided to close it. "It was lighthearted and very popular with people in the neighborhood as well as those who came downtown to eat there. When the lease was up the increase in rent would have necessitated too many compromises with what the place was about. Higher prices mean paying much closer attention to the bottom line than I like to do. I didn't want to always worry about the numbers. I really like dealing with a good environment, the food, and the people. I also like change and evolution. I had to think about what I wanted to do next and I realized that I was beginning to think perhaps I didn't want too much more red meat, cheese, and sour cream.

"I changed my diet to eat healthier things like vegetable chili, and when I tried to continue eating healthier at some of the nicer restaurants, I found few places had anything to do with healthier eating. It seemed you could distill it to three categories: 'Fun Food,' which were enjoyable places to eat, with good food but not fine food; 'Fine Dining,' places which offered wonderful food and service, but were often a little too serious to be fun; and then there were the 'health-food' restaurants, which were not often about enjoying yourself so much as healing and fueling. So I tried to put together a concept that combined the three. Eat healthily, enjoy it, and have a good time. NosmoKing opened in 1989.

"I knew I wanted to cater from the start, so that part of the business is not really very separate for us. Some of our catering customers eat at the restaurant frequently, others have never eaten at NosmoKing. First we talk about the party and then the menu. Chef Alan Harding and I do it all. We don't have a separate catering manager or chef. We show them our menu, but most of the time a party is served custom, rather than set, dishes. We are committed to seasonal changes market availability for freshness and quality and even the weather. Even though it is late October we are still having produce from the late summer harvests which won't be around in a couple of months. So we wait a couple of months before getting into the root vegetables because we will use them until April. Even for our off-premise catering we do most of the prep and cooking in our kitchen.

"Our style tends to be casual. We can be soigné and hire a captain with a headset and rent anything we need, but we prefer to do downtown, down-home dinner parties that fit into our clients' lives comfortably. Recently a good friend of a well-known painter asked us to cater a birthday party for him in her loft. We did a buffet meal for one hundred, after passing around hors d'oeuvres. We deliberately rented fewer tables and chairs so that people would walk about and talk and use the ambience of the place the party was held at.

"It isn't always a question of money, it's a matter of style. To be open to various experiences we are happy to work with people who are budget-conscious, and we put as much care into one client as the next. For sit-down dinners I prefer to keep it between forty and sixty people. But we can do it all. Location, decor, flowers, entertainment. We didn't drop into this situation fully formed. I know more this year than last.

"I interview the client, and make them think about what they want. Often they just say, 'I have to do this thing.' But you generally can get them to be specific. Don't mind explaining all the options, though some people really don't want to get involved at all. They just want it worked out for them. Usually it is better to work with the client and make it a party you've planned together, then there are no big surprises for either. Some people can't or won't handle that, and you have to go along with them.

"Don't be afraid to talk about money. I think one of the hardest things when you start out is to overcome being shy about mentioning money. I learned to ask early on in talking with a client, so I know beforehand what to present. If you start out too elaborately and then have to start taking away, the client feels they are not getting the best, when actually all kinds of parties can be good and memorable. When they refer to a price, begin to ask them what that figure includes. Is it their food and liquor budget? Is it for food only? Be as specific as you can from the start, so that you build the event, not carve away at it.

"If you are going to take the job, you should be able to make money on it. After all, that's why you are in business. The main thing is communicating with the client and transferring it to paper. Every time I have neglected to get the client to check everything on paper it has cost me money. I present a contract with a priced menu. There is a general breakdown of the cost, hors d'oeuvres, cocktails, meal, wine, dessert, coffee-service rentals, whatever. Spell it out. Then if there are questions you can be exact—this serving of hors d'oeuvres, or these wines can be eliminated or substitutes found. One client for a wedding party wanted cocktails and hot sweet hors d'oeuvres passed while the guests were waiting for the ceremony, then hot savory hors d'oeuvres served after the ceremony, and then assorted small sweets served with the coffee after the bridal cake. By itemizing, it is clear how specific items add up.

"It not only protects you, but brings you into a really good working relationship with the client."

ROBERT KINKEAD, KINKEAD'S, WASHINGTON, D.C.

Bob Kinkead, an owner and executive chef at Kinkead's, which recently opened to accolades, only does off-premise catering for charity events and fund-raisers that the restaurant genuinely believes in. "It is difficult to do off-premise what can be done in my own kitchen. Catering is mainly logistics. How do I get the food there? How will it all look? Will it be up to my standards? Will it be the right amount? Large charity events are not necessarily R.S.V.P.ed too accurately. I want the food as tasty and good looking as possible. Does the participating place have a kitchen, even a warming kitchen so that hot food can be served hot? Do we make an assortment of food that tastes best at room temperature or cold? What do we select as an offering? Overextending the kitchen diminishes quality. Since a double standard is impossible, it has to be an event we really believe in, so we choose them carefully. It must be something that raises money for a good cause, satisfies the client, gives pleasure to the guests, and reflects well on us." "Zoofari," the large fund-raiser at the Washington, D.C., Zoo, was an event Kinkead participated in when he was executive chef at the now closed Twenty One Federal. The tradition will probably continue because it is not only well run, but so much fun that the staff wants to do it.

STANLEY POLL, WILLIAM POLL CATERERS, NEW YORK

Stanley Poll, who runs William Poll Caterers in New York City, jokes that catering à la carte requires the commitment of a marriage without offering the benefits. You can go twenty-four hours a day. "Your time is not your own—and that's almost entirely preparing meals and food for pick up and delivery only." Stanley's father, William Poll, joined his brother's food business and opened a food shop in New York in the 1920s. Many residents of the Upper East Side in those days had full staffs, waiters, valets, butlers, and maids but often not a large enough kitchen to prepare the food for large parties. The clients also needed cases of this delicacy and that delectable which Poll had the resources to supply. The clientele had pretty sophisticated palates and appreciated quality food.

After World War II, domestic staffs were reduced and more people worked outside their homes. William Poll began to prepare simple quality frozen gourmet food that could be picked up on the way home. This innovation caught on with his customers. As his clients traveled further afield, to the Near East and Far East, Poll added dishes from these cuisines to his fresh frozen line. The business gradually shifted to fresh prepared food as people wanted more variety. They made dinner for the parties and special events of neighborhood people and their business grew by leaps and bounds. The menu has expanded to sixty different dinners, though they are not all available all the time. People from a tristate area will order their favorite meals from what still appears to be a small shop.

Stanley Poll stepped in when his father thought of selling and retiring. His expertise in advertising lets him understand the market. He advises people new to catering to do what they do well and create a market for it, rather than compete against everyone. "If you do a wonderful salmon, let that be your specialty. Build from there. Taking on A to Z is dangerous. If you make your base solid, you have something to build on. You need commitment, drive, and sustained energy. You also have to understand satisfying people's expectations, no changes at the last minute, and you have to be on time. Planes and trains can be late, but not dinner or, for that matter, coffee. People are driven by their appetite. They will wait hours at an airport without grumbling, but if their food isn't on the table within minutes they feel free to complain. So whatever you are doing, you have to bring quality and timing. If you advertise, do it clearly. We advertise very modestly and then people are usually very pleased when they see what we deliver."

ANNEMARIE COLBIN, THE NATURAL GOURMET COOKERY SCHOOL, NEW YORK

When asked whether it is worth the time it takes to go to school, Annemarie Colbin, the founder of The Natural Gourmet Cookery

School, says, "You learn much faster what it would take a long time to learn."

There are a growing group of people who prefer whole or "natural" foods for special occasions. Caterers don't have to specialize, but they are missing out if they don't learn about good and tasty food that is grain-based with lots of vegetables and fruit. Virtually fat-free and frequently dairy-free, these good quality nourishing dishes can be cooked in a wide range of dishes. As part of a larger palette, natural foods add the possibility of extending business for caterers who have clients who pay attention to the nutrition of every meal they eat. Both classic and ethnic dishes can be made from fresh provisions, to please any appetite. Preparing and seasoning natural foods can be as delicious and exciting as anything else on the table and to aficionados even more so. By combining textures, shapes, and colors, the various flavors are enhanced. By spending as much thought on these dishes as others it encourages people to eat a more harmonious array. Far from rigid, the school presents dietary information that affects not only physical health but emotional states as well.

Annemarie Colbin encourages students to do things that make sense to them, not because someone tells them to do it. She has been successfully independent in her teaching and writing. Many people talk rather medicinally about food and health but the Whole Meal Course at the school features gourmet applications for professional chefs as well as beginners. As researchers are finding out more about nutrition and the mysterious immune system, there is nothing to be lost by increasing the grains and vegetables in our diets.

There are also fewer sanitation problems and very little waste. At a buffet you can serve two or three dishes from the natural foods menu. Seaweed salad, whole grain pilaf, and soup are good examples. If caterers learn the basics of whole foods cooking and perhaps take a course in desserts that use fruits poached or baked and sweetened with natural syrups, they broaden their culinary horizons.

FRANCOIS DIONOT, L'ACADEMIE DE CUISINE, BETHESDA, MARYLAND

Francois Dionot, chef extraordinaire and director of L'Academie de Cuisine, says the hardest thing on the first job you are responsible for is the unexpected.

"The most difficult thing at the beginning is to anticipate all the little things that are going to go wrong. We find out it is never the same as the last time. It is not like when people come to you, as in a restaurant. We take food to somebody's house and every time we serve different things to different people there are crazy unknowns. It's what makes it exciting. An example. It happened to me once. Beautiful house where the reception has begun when I arrive. Band playing, photographers taking pictures, everyone having a good time. I plug my coffee urn into a socket and blow everything up. The band is using electricity, the photographer is using it, but I am the last one to arrive and so I am responsible.

"The unknown is what happens even when we think we are prepared. To be extremely organized is most important. It's like a pilot before takeoff. Double-check everything each time and don't assume things are fine. If you forget to check, it increases the chance of crashing.

"Presenting and plating food comes from experience. You can study and devour books and magazines and look at pictures for ideas, but it is practice that gives direction. You can't decorate food before knowing how to cook. After learning about food and becoming confident with preparing and serving, you build style as your understanding grows.

"When you are starting out in catering a strong education in all culinary arts, not necessarily just in catering, is essential. A minimal would be an intensive six months to learn to do professional basics. After that, make the transition to as good a cooking job as you can get in a restaurant or catering practice. The basic food ideas are the same, but transported at the last minute.

"My experience is cooking first and then catering. It has served me best for everything. A chef must have not only a good general knowledge, but must understand timing which you can apply to other things.

"It is possible, but very difficult, to be full-fledged when you first start out. If you don't already have a specialty or a preference, choose one. Make soups and salads for example, then make the soups and salads available. Just sell hors d'oeuvres or desserts. Whether your clients pick these things up or you deliver them, they have to be your best.

"On your first job for a wedding of 250, become a general contractor. Hire things out. Don't think of baking the cake yourself unless that is all you are making. The client is hiring *you*. You don't have to tell them your resources. You take the credit and the blame. If you have built a network, you can make the client happy. There is always a way to do it or find someone to do it.

"Learn to manage time. If the caterer finds themself alone washing pots and pans at 2 A.M., they did not plan well. A young business should hire from the start. It doesn't make sense not to. Help is part of what you have to organize so you are not burned out.

"Start by buying only basic catering equipment and every time you need to do something special, then you buy the necessary pieces. If a party requires two thousand crepes, then you buy crepe pans. You can rent practically anything, but most people feel more comfortable with dependable equipment in their possession. There are successful caterers who rent everything almost all the time. It is best to buy the things you use frequently and have strong preferences for.

"Your main marketing device is word of mouth. Make sure whatever you do, you do so well that everyone will want you for their next job.

"To attract attention, create an event, either for charity or a celebration. You might arrange with somebody who has a beautiful home for them to invite friends and include the press. Make it a special event or even a special day, but don't call it a demonstration.

Perhaps you can invite a celebrity. The caterer foots the food bill and gets exposure you can't get just from advertising or letter writing.

"Catering means to cater to whatever the customer wants. Even one person's special needs have to be met. If the client says one guest is a vegetarian, make a lovely vegetable dish. There should be many alternative dishes possible for you as a chef that won't cost much and are easy, but wonderful. Don't be reluctant to extend yourself. That is what will build your business. Sometimes the host is vegetarian, or has a dietary need, so prepare something special for them and serve others normally. Pay attention to special requests and then people will talk about you as 'my caterer.'

"Be very catering. Give, if somebody asks you for something, give and you give a little bit more, say an assortment of truffles not on the bill, or an extra hor d'oeuvre, not on the bill. It isn't costly because there is always food in the commissary we can use. Everyone likes a treat, so put in a little extra. Tell the client, 'I couldn't resist doing this—it is a favorite of mine—I wanted to make it for your party.' It isn't the price, especially for people who are graciously paying a large bill. It is an insight into human nature. Everyone likes a little something given to them. Make it something different each time and your clients will call you back."

PROFESSIONALS INTERVIEWED

Annemarie Colbin
The Natural Gourmet Cookery School
48 West 21 Street, 2nd floor
New York, NY 10010
Phone: (212) 645-5170

Ronnie Davis
Washington Street Cafe
433 Washington Street
New York, NY 10013
Phone: (800) 338-3977; (212) 925-5119 /
Fax: (212) 041-8326

Francois Dionot
L'Academie de Cuisine
5021 Wolson Lane
Bethesda, MD 20814
Phone: (800) 445-1959; (301) 986-9490 /
Fax: (301) 652-7970

Steve Frankel
NosmoKing
54 Varick Street
New York, NY 10013
Phone: (212) 966-1239

Jonathan Horst
Adobo Catering
1807 Second Street
Santa Fe, NM 87501
Phone: (505) 989-7674

Robert Kinkead
Kinkead's
2000 Pennsylvania Ave., N.W.
Washington, DC 20006
Phone: (202) 296-7700

Joe McDonnal
  Market Place Caterers
  3001 East Yesler Way
  Seattle, WA
  Phone: (206) 324-5900

Jim McMullen
  Jim McMullen's Restaurant and Catering
  1341 Third Avenue
  New York, NY 10021
  Phone: (212) 861-4700

Jacques Pepin, Dean of Studies
  French Culinary Institute
  462 Broadway
  New York, NY 10013
  Phone: (212) 219-8890

Stanley Poll
  William Poll Caterers
  1051 Lexington Avenue
  New York, NY 10023
  Phone: (212) 288-0501

Sylvia Weinstock
  Sylvia Weinstock's Cakes
  273 Church Street
  New York, NY 10013
  Phone: (212) 925-4430

FOUR

The Business Office

Sole proprietor is the designation of most start-up catering entre-preneurs. The good news and the bad news are identical—the profits and losses are all yours.

Partnerships are rarely formed because they are structured as if two people were sole proprietors, with each subject to responsibility for the other. Sometimes a limited partnership is chosen because it usually protects the investing partners from losing anything more than their original investment should any serious liability be in-curred. Neither form of partnership is as generally useful for small businesses as forming a corporation. As with any situation de-manding legal options, you must write a clear list of your intentions, needs, and questions, and have a lawyer review them with you. It might be a good time to get the services of an accountant as well. Each decision you make carries federal and state tax, insurance, and legal liability ramifications.

By far the most popular way to set up a small business is cur-rently the S corporation. Again, you must speak to a lawyer and accountant about these things, but the general advantages of an S corporation are that your personal assets are not liable should your company run into credit problems. And although there is a lot more paperwork, you are taxed similarly to a sole proprietorship—only on personal earnings. Though you may have up to thirty-five share-holders, all stock must be of the same class and you must keep your books in time with the calendar year. Initially your expenses are the small fees involved in becoming incorporated, company-name approval, and your corporate charter and seal. These fees, for a small start-up business, can usually be figured in hundreds, not thousands, of dollars, so it is generally well worth it. There are small annual fees, but they also help you think of your catering business as a separate financial entity, about which you can make goal-oriented decisions.

The C corporation is something your lawyer and accountant will advise you about if they feel your capital and business structure demand it. It requires full-blown corporate action and often cumbersome document and tax work as well as increased expenses. You may also want to ask your lawyer about an LLC, which is a Limited Liability Corporation. This structure is gaining favor and has been approved by several states since the IRS said it was an acceptable corporate option. It may serve to give you both the tax advantages of a proprietorship and the liability advantages of a corporation. The important thing is to ask a lot of questions of experienced people and organizations, and explain your goals as clearly as you can. Remember, even though you need, and the law requires, licensed professionals to perform certain legal and financial duties, you are the one who must shape a business you are happy with.

Service Corporation of Retired Executives (SCORE), in Washington D.C., offers free consultations to start-up businesses. And the Answer Desk at the Small Business Administration will take your calls.

COLLECTING FINANCIAL INFORMATION

One of the things that can be done as you start to create the files that will eventually be your office is to put together a personal financial resume. It will lead to finding the net worth on which you can base your financial plan. Collect the following asset and liability information: house property, house contents, kitchen and office contents, investments, bank accounts, Keoghs, IRAs, personal assets and debts, loans outstanding, mortgages, unpaid taxes, and so on. These figures will at least give you a starting point. This is a place to be as realistic as possible. Your personal assets will probably be the foundation of your business.

Your next resource might be personal loans and credit from banks. Should you seek loans from friends and family, common sense will dictate it would be only after you have had some experience and done a fair amount of research and development. Even though it might not seem necessary with friends and family, you will be well advised to write up a letter describing the loan, the amount, and the conditions and time frame for paying it back.

Once you determine what your operating fund is, you really have to shepherd your assets well. Off-premise catering is not a business that venture capitalists will get involved with. It rarely shows enough profitability to pay back the $4 to $10, per dollar, of their investment within five years, which is their usual expectation. And rarely is the income or liquidity enough at any single point to reclaim the stake of investment bankers. Even after several years of being financially stable and maintaining good credit, it is unlikely that you will be able to raise an enormous new infusion of money. So overextending is a bad business plan.

For assets like a refrigerated truck or other equipment, the manufacturer can often be helpful in financing. Eventually your business should have good enough credit to cover the need for expansion or new equipment.

If you are turned down for a loan to which you think you might be entitled, the Small Business Administration—which does not itself lend money—may consider guaranteeing your loan from the bank. They will guarantee a maximum of 90 percent up to $155,000 and 85 percent to a maximum of $750,000. Your personal profile, a very good description of your market, collateral, and payback plan must be presented with a solid three-year proposal, though the loan does not necessarily have to be paid back in that time.

When approaching a professional for capital, there is a ten to twenty times better chance at success if the business has been operating for several years with some accomplishment and profit. You will get more attention if your story is one about a business ready to take off, than one starting from scratch. As in catering itself, a lot depends on you. Investors want to hear a truly good scenario and projection about why you want a couple of hundred thousand dollars when your business only makes fifty thousand dollars a year. Show convincingly that this investment will turn your company into a million-dollar business and people will listen. You will have to show a very good track record, personally and professionally, and offer a specific plan—whether it is buying banquet facilities, an old inn, or a food processing facility.

Going this route, you yourself have to be convinced that 50 to 75 percent of your business will be worth more than the 100 percent that you have now. Major investors want not only a higher yield on something risky but want to be a part of it. "Can I do it?" and "Do I want to do it?" are the questions to be asked twice each time you consider taking on bigger financial obligations.

SELECTING INSURANCE

You will need some insurance as your lawyer advises you. It is better to work with an insurance broker when you are a small business. Generally speaking, an agent gets bonuses from insurance companies for sales, and a broker earns most of their money looking out for your interests. Try to find a small brokerage house in your area and explain your needs. The big ones only handle really large accounts and you will not be well served. A small brokerage firm can handle not only product liability, but general fire and theft, vehicle, and equipment, to say nothing of Workers' Compensation insurance which is something that is required and regulated state by state.

Brokers shop around the insurance companies to see who is going to cover this risk in the best and most economical way. It is necessary to learn all the insurance you are responsible for. Some people will not buy food from you without a food insurance number, and others will not let you operate on their premises without insurance for property damage. Most of the brand-name foods you use have Broad Form Vendors Endorsements attached to their own policies, but it will be necessary for you to protect yourself. These days you cannot even leave samples at most places without a certificate of product liability. As people become more and more food conscious and aware of the relationship of food to health, they are wary of food, the source, and handling of which they are unsure. Most people who have come into catering after years of cooking for friends, family, and other large groups resent this, but the professional network is acknowledging the need for insurance and regards it as a necessary operating business expense and figure it is part of their overhead. It is not an area in which to be penny wise and pound foolish. Your thoroughness in researching this area will be well rewarded.

Given the enormous amount of food produced in this country, industry standards are remarkably high, and though you might fear a lot of risk, there are relatively few claims in this area. Some insurance costs will be an annual overhead amount and others will be for specific jobs that have to be figured into your profitability analysis.

You might want cancellation insurance that protects both the host and the caterer for the loss of the deposit and the profit, usually up to about $25,000. There are also some companies that will insure a caterer on a per-event basis against the failure to produce promised services, like the band or a tent. Though some on-site compromises are made, a client can sometimes sue for general pain and suffering caused by a breach of contract.

Kornreich Insurance Services in New York is one place that has developed a program exclusively for caterers. A large business, even a start-up, has more options than a small one, and often a young business does not even think about insurance until there is a snag that requires it. Speak with your lawyer. The program for caterers that Kornreich has outlined addresses this category and broadly analyzes it. There is some cost saving and buying strength in being part of a newly recognized insurance segment. The insurance industry is in great flux and various plans from various companies will have to be reviewed. If you are stuck, Kornreich will work with your agent or broker, and if you do not have one, will suggest one in your area.

The Insurance Information Institute is a nonprofit resource that will answer your specific insurance questions. How do I insure this? For how much? What do I need to start? Their member companies get data base news daily. They will direct callers to facts and figures that are guides to selecting coverage. As always in these matters, speak with your agent or broker, and your lawyer. Regulations have some variables and you want to make an informed and legally correct decision.

SETTING UP YOUR BUSINESS

Most people would be surprised to see that many million-dollar businesses are run from spaces no larger than their bedroom. One of the advantages of starting an off-premise catering business is that you can begin at whatever level of investment you are comfortable with and achieve success. A desk, table, a few chairs, files, shelves, and a reliable telephone, fax, and answering machine are probably more than enough for starters. Your computer and software will be your biggest office expense.

A conventional personal computer with a hard drive and 3.5 and 5.25 ancillary drives is your best bet. Get one with the largest hard drive and memory you can afford and by and large it will enable you to add additional stations, interact with other users, and try new software that interests you. Word-processing systems abound. The advantages of using industry giants such as WordPerfect® or Windows™ are their commitment to general utility, their excellent telephone support systems, and their popularity. Almost everyone you hire to work at the computer will have encountered one or both programs. You can also convert almost any other system to be used with them. It is practical to start out with a computer because you will start building correspondence and information files immediately.

It is also good training in keeping things simple and orderly. If you keep one hard copy of important documents and back up your system files frequently, even a novice keyboarder will be well pleased with the assistance of a computer. If you expect someone else will be using it, there is equal reason to have one, as any changes and additions to anything you want can be produced momentarily. If you plan on producing your own menus and flyers, you might want a color printer, but it is not necessary and you can always buy one later on.

The expenses of such general office supplies as business cards, letterhead stationary, and labels with your logo that can go on presentation folders will be pretty minimal compared to telephone and other communications expenses.

KEEPING TRACK OF FINANCES

With a minimum of paperwork, a little filing, and a good deal of patience you can keep track of expenses, income, and profit. If you start out with a simple clear system and make the time to keep it up to date, you will always know where you stand. Business is one place you want your right hand to know what your left is doing. Whether by inclination you lean toward being openhanded or tight-fisted, the paper trail you create will lead to a clear and comprehensive view of what your financial position is at any time.

There are many easy bookkeeping methods and computer systems that will help you. A simple ledger with items entered as you pay or receive them will do the trick. Several envelopes for cash receipts, rent, telephone, utilities, balanced checkbooks, and credit-card statements will tell you almost everything you need to know. When you get really busy there are many free-lance bookkeepers who will work one day or more per week or per month. Ask your accountant what system he or she suggests for record keeping. You will be able to forecast your needs as you become able to separate your permanent overhead, various business outlays, and specific job costs. Whether restrained or extravagant in business, or a little of each, it is necessary at all times to have realistic information so you can get and give good value.

Your accountant will tell you what sales taxes are applicable in your region. You will probably also need IRS and state employer I.D. numbers and a resale number. Playing ostrich in this area could expose you to fines and penalties that are more costly than paying correctly in the first place. And the stress reduction is enormous.

CHOOSING YOUR STAFF

Good teamwork between office, kitchen, and service staffs is essential for a pleasant and productive workplace. Often people will have to pinch hit. Even office staff must be service-oriented and relate well to people. Positive and cheerful people, who are solution minded, are as important in the office as off-premise. Office flexibility will be as important as kitchen flexibility. Ideally, you will be surrounded by independent people who are team players.

USING COMPUTER SOFTWARE

Computer systems vary from very user-friendly to levels of complexity that require training sessions. By the time you contact the software companies listed, the programs they offer will certainly have been changed. The basic strategies will remain the same, but the rule of thumb is that they are constantly upgraded, in a way that can be integrated into the program you are already using. All software companies have people who will answer your questions. If you are one of those who thrive in the kitchen but are reluctant to get involved with computers—get over it! Given a choice, it may be better to employ a person than a machine, but it is no longer an either/or condition. Good software has enhanced working conditions so that more jobs can be taken on and give more employment in the foodservice industry beyond fast food. Computers help with word processing, accounting, food measures, and pricing. A fax capacity is handy to send memos, confirmations, and shopping lists without generating duplicated paper. But for sending printed documents not on your computer and general fax exchanges, a separate fax machine is also necessary.

Scan phones and shopping by computer are available in some regions and not in others and may or may not suit you or your business style. There are computer modem systems like Compu-Serve® that have informational networks, but the novice can run up some big bills as they charge by the minute.

Lotus' simplest bookkeeping system is 1-2-3 Home™. It benefits from years of getting the glitches out of the popular Lotus 1-2-3®, another recommended start-up program. It will take a little learning, but Lotus offers not only written manuals, but on-line support. It also comes with what they call SmartSheets™—preprogrammed invoices, agendas, accounts payable and receivable, network, and bank balancing sheets. If you are purchasing only one system, this one makes sense because its popularity assures that you will find someone to operate it more than competently. It also has the capacity to be converted to use with a variety of systems. Most schools in your area will offer a few hours of instruction.

EATEC™ is a system that has a particular plan for caterers that even start-up entrepreneurs would benefit from. The Catering System's main menu lets you enter an order and update it, do an event cost analysis, and keep track of equipment and beverage recipes suited for off-premise situations. It will also let you do catering accounting by opening client receivables as well as all categories of payables. They are keyed into both a standard accounting number, such as #2120 for accounts payable, and your in-house numbers as well. Suppliers are listed by name and category, produce, beverage, poultry, baked goods, paper, cleaning supplies, and so forth. It will let you balance several checkbooks and control petty cash. You can generate menus and recipes and scale and price them. It will also give the nutrition information most people are interested in: calories, proteins, carbohydrates, various fats, cholesterol, sodium, and potassium.

EATEC™ is a system that can be used as simply as you want and grow with your business. It is DOS-based, networkable, and IBM-compatible. The general ledger worksheets can be handled by anyone who can learn a debit from a credit. Its catering features let you easily break events down into components that can be priced according to their details and put together for a client presentation. It is a good negotiating tool because you can easily see what can be added, changed, or deleted. It also helps you generate several options that you can offer clients when they call for similar events like weddings or fund-raisers. It gives you the opportunity to offer fixed-price menus and allows you to set up beverage packages. You can quickly see the difference in equipment rentals for sit-down dinners and buffets.

"The Recipe Writer Pro" is an effective software program that allows you to scale recipes and cost them in a consistent fashion. It offers a lot of on-screen help that is good for busy people. You can generate a number of recipes, limited only by the size of your hard disk. You can combine recipes like sauces and dressings simply by calling them up into new ones. You can print recipes with or without prices and notes, and generate shopping lists.

For people who put nutrition first, there is no better system than Esha Research's "Food Processor" programs. For institutional caterers and people planning food careers that are nutrient data-based, or for people who wish to incorporate increasing amounts of recommended and researched analysis, the food list includes raw and cooked plain items like chicken breast with skin, chicken breast without skin, and prepared foods like cheesecake or condensed cream of mushroom soup. It comes compatible with IBM or Macintosh systems. It will calculate nutrients in single foods and recipes, or if you are packaging foods at all or even making samples, it will give measurements in both metric and standard household portions.

"Dine Right" seems best suited for people who are combining food and fitness. It is a bit specific for an off-premise caterer starting up. "Dine Right" has a list of the number of calories burned in about two hundred activities including swimming (which is broken down into backstroke, fast/slow, breaststroke, fast/slow, etc.), in addition to the food values of almost six thousand items, with caloric and nutrient information of those commercially prepared and at fast-food franchises.

"Nutritionist IV" is a good "Spa" cuisine guide. It will tell you the contents of ten forms of orange juice. It has many dietary components and will even generate diabetic food exchanges. "Nutritionist IV" has recipes for things like no-cholesterol soy mayonnaise and it allows for additional information to be added and amended. It is best to use this if you have taken at least a couple of courses in special nutrition and want to create special meals, if needed. It will analyze a day's food or a week's recipes with the RDA of food components and recommend a menu for a specific calorie count.

BUSINESS DIRECTORY

Blumberg Legal Forms
62 White Street
New York, NY 10013
Phone: (212) 431-5000

College of Insurance
101 Murray Street
New York, NY 10007
Phone: (212) 962-4111

Insurance Information Institute
110 William Street
New York, NY 10038
Phone: (212) 669-9200

Kornreich Insurance Services
919 Third Avenue
New York, NY 10022
Phone: (212) 688-9700; (800) 321-2122
Fax: (212) 319-7509

SBA
   U.S. Small Business Administration
   House of Representatives
   2361 Rayburn House Office Building
   Washington, DC 20515-0315
   Phone: (800) U-ASK-SBA Answer Desk

Service Corporation of Retired Executives
   1825 Connecticut Avenue, N.W., Suite 508
   Washington, DC 20009
   Phone: (202) 653-6279
   (SCORE offers free consultations to start-up businesses)

Triple S, Incorporated
   Insurance Administration for the Food Processing Industry
   1401 New York Avenue, N.W., Suite 400
   Washington, DC 20005
   Phone: (202) 628-4435

COMPUTER SOFTWARE

At-Your-Service Software, Inc.
   "The Recipe Writer Pro"
   450 Bronxville Road
   Bronxville, NY 10708
   Phone: (914) 337-9030

EATEC Corporation
   2904 San Pablo Avenue
   Berkeley, CA 94702
   Phone: (510) 548-1810 / Fax: (510) 549-1959

ESHA Research
   P.O. Box 13028
   Salem, OR 97309
   Phone: (503) 585-6242 / Fax: (503) 585-5543

Lotus Development Corporation
55 Cambridge Parkway
Cambridge, MA 02142

N^2 *Computing*
3040 Commercial Street S.E., Suite 240
Salem, OR 97302
Phone: (503) 364-9270

Dine Systems, Inc.
"Dine Right"
586 French Road, Suite 2
Amherst, NY 14228
Phone: (716) 688-2492 / Fax: (716) 688-2505

United States Department of Labor
Office of the Assistant Secretary for Policy
200 Constitution Avenue, N.W.
Washington, DC 20210
Phone: (202) 219-6197
TDD Phone: (800) 326-2577
(Small Business Handbook:
Laws Regulations and Technical Assistance Service)

The Hermann Group
Mindy Hermann, Nutritionist/Computer Analyst
50 Barker Street
Mt. Kisco, NY 10549
Phone: (914) 241-8714

Managing an Event from Introduction to Conclusion (Including Contracts and Worksheets)

Interviewing is one of the most important parts of a caterer's job. From the interview will be learned exactly what the client wants, not just the facts but the spirit of the expectations that will have to be met.

There will be a lot of flowery descriptions and breathless fantasies that have to be translated into shopping lists, budgets, time schedules, labor, delivery, setup, serving, and cleanup. You are going to have to decide how much of a professional team is needed and how it is best coordinated. Most of the time the client not only doesn't want to do the work themselves but doesn't even want to think of the work that has to be done. Magic is part of the calculation. Everything has to be presented in as gracious and reassuring a manner you can muster. Many caterers have a certain amount of stage fright all the time.

Whether you intend to deliver à la carte, full service, or somewhere in the middle, the first large professional job you get will probably be a private party. You may not believe it now but planning for one hundred people will soon seem like a small number. The need for a relaxed sense of organization cannot be emphasized enough. It is your client's stress that you have to deal with. They will fret and worry because most private clients do not use caterers often, and usually it is for a special celebration that has emotional overtones. They want not only a wonderful time and a delicious meal but fine memories, photos, and video opportunities.

Forget your wishes of someone handing you a blank check to create the meal of your choice in the place of your choice. It is your job to provide a service that pleases and suits each client. If you think you cannot deliver, it is better to say no than to do a shoddy job.

You will have to decide what area to highlight. If it is a birthday party, a simple meal and expensive cake might be in order. For a business lunch, the most expensive ingredients would be your main course with just a light dessert. It sometimes helps to ask around for the going rate among other caterers. You don't want to create a conflict because established caterers are not thrilled when you undercut them, but by the same token, a tyro simply cannot command the prices of well-known pros. Analyze the competition and try to start out being fair, as this is a community where goodwill is important. You don't want to be "the cheap one" and you want to deliver a truly professional product. Also, you don't want to commit to a price range you can't maintain. The odds are that if it can't be delivered at the price your client wants, no one else will do it either.

The client will undoubtedly want to know the per-person cost of the food and the easiest way to do this is to have a simple breakdown for the dishes you prepare the most often, using average fair-market prices. The exact price may vary pennies a pound from week to week but to refigure labor costs each week would add more to the price of each item. Any radical changes will, of course, be reflected in your prices.

When you figure the cost of the prepared food, it is before it leaves your kitchen or commissary. If your client wishes to pick it up at that point you simply have to use your profit multiplier and write the bill. A general figure is "times 4." Overhead staff time will be at least—$10 to $15 an hour. When you factor wages, be sure that in addition to specific fees paid to you, your own time is never figured at less than double the minimum wage for any aspect of the work you perform. This sounds silly at first, but when you think that you will be planning and revising, comparison shopping, interviewing staff, scouting locations, doing promotional and public relations work a good deal, and not able to earn other money at the same time, your business has to be personally cost efficient.

Figure pantry costs either on a use-to-use basis—five cents a dish for salt and pepper, for example—or as part of your overhead. If the commissary pantry is stocked with staple items, you might try to keep a running tally of costs for the first year to get an accurate picture of what your must-haves cost, and how best to be reimbursed for them. Often a general pantry cost is best because when you have different preparers the charge will be consistent.

Other kitchen expenses, like pots and pans and other cooking equipment, are factored in. If it is necessary to buy a new utensil for a specific event, the client cannot be charged for it, but it is figured in proportionally.

Someone who has been a guest at a dinner party or perhaps a charity event you volunteered for has approached you to do a wedding party for about a hundred guests at their home and garden at 2 P.M. the afternoon of Saturday, the fifteenth of June. It is February and you are free on that date, so you arrange to meet with the client or clients.

Even though you may be meeting with a family who have to be pleased as a group, it is necessary to ascertain who is in charge. Perhaps it is the bridal couple. Traditionally it has been the bride's parents, but it could be the groom's, or both. If there is more than one person, you will have to get them to be clear about who will be their spokesperson. For social catering your interpersonal skills will be your greatest preproduction asset. The others are the details of beginning-to-end planning.

You have the date, time, and the nature of the event. It might save time by having the first meeting at the site of the party. Feel free to bring an assistant who will make a checklist of available prep, cooking, and warming utilities as well as cold storage. It is necessary to see how much can actually be cooked on-site. Will professional pans fit in the oven and storage facilities? Where will the dirty dishes, glasses, and pots go? Busing and cleaning schedules and assignments are as important as shopping and cooking towards managing a successful event. Are there any special requirements, pets, children? Ask clients what can be used, from equipment to special serving pieces. Walk through the spaces, both back of the house and party area. Ask if there are location restrictions. Ask about bathrooms and if they want someone to attend them—do they need a portable unit rented? Is there adequate parking and do they want a valet? Will they notify the police about the excess traffic and perhaps noise?

You need to know the event agenda and the general style. Another advantage of visiting them is that you can get a feeling for their preferences: formal; casual; traditional; adventurous; quiet; noisy.

Will there be a ceremony? Is it the caterer's job to create the area for the service? Will the event be held rain or shine? Are tents required? Who will be there to grant access on-site a day or two before and, if necessary, the day after the event? Will they be responsible for equipment left there before and/or after the event?

What kind of food service? Butlered hot hors d'oeuvres and perhaps a service buffet with guests seated at set tables is one possibility that requires a minimum of wait staff. Sometimes a Russian service, where food is presented on a platter and a server puts the portion on each guest's plate, is used. Soup or a salad can be served this way while the main course is being individually plated in the kitchen for service American style. For your first big party you might set up food at various buffet stations, with servers at each large dish who help the guests to dinner in what is sometimes referred to as a modified British service.

After much discussion, you select a menu that includes a large selection of various hot hors d'oeuvres, cold platters, and a buffet of poached salmons with cucumber-horseradish sauce, naturally cured hams served with assorted chutneys and custom mustards, roasted mini-vegetables with lemon-mint butter, wild rice, a tossed field salad with edible flowers and Hampton Dressing. The bread baskets will contain herb and corn biscuits. There will be a stand-up cocktail hour with some hors d'oeuvre stations and some, fresh from the oven, butlered on trays. Wine, beer, and various soft drinks and waters will be at two bars, one inside and one outside. There will be a champagne toast served on trays by the wait staff. The wedding cake, berries and cream, and chocolate truffles will be for dessert. Coffee, both regular and decaf, as well as a variety of teas will be at an attended station after dinner.

Staff suggestions might work out to be: two for bar service, who will also set up, keep glasses filled during dinner and help clear after the guests leave; and a kitchen manager who is a good cook and will work in the commissary the day before the party as well, and will direct off-premise food flow with a wait staff of three. They will help set up, pass hors d'oeuvres, serve buffet stations, and help pick up after guests leave.

The clients will take care of hiring the photographer and musicians and will set up the outdoor lighting. They will also arrange for a private carter to remove the garbage which has only to be tied in heavy-duty bags. They want no tent but would like a small dance floor. Their colors are navy blue, orchid, and pink, and they would like small centerpieces on ten tables, but will order the bridal flowers themselves. They do not want assigned seats.

In off-premise catering there are more consequences when a detail is overlooked or a glitch in equipment or product occurs. Backup is usually some distance away. The importance of planning and prepping cannot be overstated since when you begin you work each job in a new environment with a costly staff unfamiliar with each other and the location. After some experience this simply turns each event into a party with exciting possibilities for creative touches. It also means that you rely heavily on the subcontractors you choose. Most beginners think the only way to deal with this is to do everything themselves. They are just delaying the inevitable and it is often better to start subcontracting early on, so that when you take on a large event you know your sources and know who you can count on.

Not only estimated prices for the different variables discussed but the manner of payment must all be put on paper. Deposits and cancellation fees are included as well. It is often reassuring to discuss small details with clients. What are the arrangements for staff meals? Will the musicians be eating, and where and when? Do they want leftovers? Caterers traditionally remove leftovers rather than leave it with the client because they are no longer responsible for the condition or maintenance of the food. If the client wants any remaining prepared food they must sign a waiver, releasing the caterer from any liability for this food. They should also sign a waiver for the food brought to the event by themselves or their guests.

Think of the personnel needed. If you are the party planner and head chef, you will need a cook who is also a kitchen manager and an assistant who will shop and prep. Both of them can also tend primary buffet stations. Three waitpersons, two bartenders, and one buser will also help set up, clean up, and pack. You may also need a dishwasher. With rented equipment you probably just have to scrape and rinse, so with everyone pitching in you can eliminate that job. Make a list and calculate the number of hours each person has to work, then add 10 percent for the estimate and a 17 percent gratuity. Properly briefed, with this kind of staff, off-premise unpacking kitchen prep and setup should not take more than two and a half hours for everyone. The length of the event will be three to four hours. Cleanup, packing, and loading will take about two hours. Salaries for the day of the event will be about twelve hundred dollars plus, and for the two days prior, six hundred dollars plus. Gratuities will be added to the bill.

In New York the cost of renting chairs varies, but the average is $4 each; tables for ten about $8 each; tablecloths about $15; napkins 75 cents each. You can inquire from local clubs and organizations and find lower prices if you have time to examine the furniture first. You will, of course, have to figure how many tables and cloths are needed for service stations. If there is none available at the location, you will need at least two for the bar and two for hors d'oeuvres, which can be cleared and set up for dessert, and three for main courses. They should be dressed as prettily as the dining tables, as they are part of the environment you are creating.

Most rental places also have side towels, aprons, and uniforms, too, if they are required. Almost any unit of china or glassware is 50 cents; champagne flutes, 85 cents; flatware, about $3 a place setting. Assorted chafing dishes and serving pieces might be another $100 and the dance floor another few hundred dollars. Clearly these prices vary from neighborhood to neighborhood, but it is good to see in black and white that everything does cost something. One of the most common errors of start-up businesses is forgetting that each and every item must be priced, often perceived as insignificant details. Catering is a business of details—the fresh herbs for the soup, the price of the herbs, adding the herbs to the soup, and adding the price to the bill. This does not mean a caterer cannot be generous. In fact, it is a good idea to give a little something like an extra hors d'oeuvre or another flavored miniature muffin for the bread basket. List it on your bill as "No Charge" and your goodwill will be appreciated.

You will order the ten centerpieces and some decorative table arrangements for the buffet tables from a florist with navy, orchid, and pink in mind and have them delivered to the location the morning of the event. Some flowers and leaves for dressing the food platters should be ordered as well.

When you begin calculating the price, think of the cost of food and the price at which it leaves the commissary; beverages; labor; rental; floral; transportation; disposables; office; gratuities; and taxes, if applicable.

After the meeting, write the client a gracious, clear, and concise letter. Reiterate your meeting and offer only a few options. Describe what and how you will deliver, and offer a price estimate. If you yourself are not going to be present or will be there for only part of the time, specify who will supervise the event and make introductions early on. It may take a couple of additions and deletions, but on receipt of a signed confirmation letter, send a contract with additional sheets relating to menus and services.

A 50 percent deposit is required on signing the contract and the balance is due the day of the function. Make clear that revisions are permitted up to two weeks preceding the event. After that time there might be a ten percent error allowance for both client and caterer.

For one hundred people with various hors d'oeuvres, two ounces of cheese per person is usually more than enough. It adds up to twelve and a half pounds. You might want to divide it into a selection: one whole wheel of Brie will be served baked with a hazelnut crust, and a half wheel each Edam and white Vermont Cheddar will be served with seedless grapes. Two fourteen-ounce chèvre logs will be used in phyllo cups with sun-dried tomatoes and one and a half pounds blue cheese will be mixed with toasted chopped walnuts for mini pâte à choux puffs. Six baguettes will make up into about two hundred crostini. To complete the hors d'oeuvres, add two big baskets of crudités with herbed yogurt dip served in hollow round peasant breads. Two hundred caviar-and-cream-cheese pinwheels. Three pounds of Prosciutto and about ten melons, ten pounds of shrimp and dips, and miniature steamed dumplings and ginger sauce. Two twenty-pound hams will run about $50 each; three ten-pound salmon might be $60 each; wild rice and mushrooms, $50; vegetables, $75; mustards, $10; and chutneys, $30. Figure closely the costs of the flour, oil and vinegar, dips, sauces, and hors d'oeuvres ingredients, as well as cake, desserts, and beverages. Factoring at "times 4" after you make a detailed list will give you the food cost. This can be done with a pencil and paper and a calculator, or it is a good time to start using your computer. If you are not accustomed to one, the awkwardness you feel at first will quickly be rewarded with the ease of success at repeated tasks.

If you are catering an event like a wedding dinner, where a good deal of food is expected, remember the rule of thumb is a minimum of one and a maximum of one and a half pounds of food per person. Calculating approximately twenty ounces will leave plenty of leeway for various appetites. Quantity is your responsibility. Even a frugal host expects volume. If they insist on pâté with a low budget, slice it thin and serve half an ounce on warm crostini on a bed of minced frisée lettuce with a mustard dressing. This way, six pounds of pâté will be more than enough. Instead of sides of smoked salmon, create a mousse of salmon, smoked salmon, and salmon roe, served in thumb-sized tartlets.

The pros all agree that there is no set schedule you can arrange and then fill in the blanks. Each event has to be done on a count-down basis after the initial strategy is settled upon. Planning should take no more than one to two days for a complicated event. The key is the person in charge. If the event is on a Saturday, everything you need, except the bread, should certainly be in the commissary by Wednesday evening or Thursday morning. On Thursday, all subcontractors and rentals that have been ordered earlier must be reconfirmed. Check with the client to make sure everything is ready on their end. If you have any doubts about staffing, this is the day to double-check.

When you are just beginning you will have to work your calendar counting down from the date of the event. You need a plan and a specifically detailed checklist under your supervision.

Even Ridgewell's Caterer, which has been in business for over fifty years and done presidential inaugural events, does not use a single formal schedule sheet. The company was started in 1928 by Charles Ridgewell, who came to Washington, D.C., as the British Ambassador's caterer and his wife, Marguerite, who had been on staff at the French Embassy. The responsibility for timing everything is up to you—the party manager—or the event executive responsible for a specific occasion. Though they have done many inaugurations and everything from the Begin–Sadat peace treaty to the opening of Union Station, Ridgewell's practice and experience have taught them that particulars at different locations and at different times of the year vary. No uniform prefixed schedule is possible.

If you put a reliable network in place and stay on top of orchestrating events, things will all come together within twenty-four to forty-eight hours of the date, usually not before that. Catering is a business that shows its success at the time of delivery.

Hampton Caterers

222 Ocean Street / Metropolis, USA 10011
Phone   123-456-7890   Fax   123-456-7890

CATERING CONTRACT

Date _____   Invoice # _____
Client _____   Client File # _____
Billing Address _____   Telephone—Day_____
_____   Telephone—Night _____
Host _____   Event _____
Location _____   Date of Event _____
_____   Time of Event _____
Hampton Coordinator_____   Type of Function _____

Confirmed guest count _____ will be guaranteed by _____
Please note and initial—Client will be billed for guaranteed or actual count, whichever is greater.

Event Schedule
Guests Arrive _____
Bar and Hors D'Oeuvres *(see attached)* _____
Lunch/Dinner *(see attached)* _____
Dessert/Cake *(see attached)* _____
Music *(see attached)* _____
Special *(see attached)* _____
Conclusion _____

Event Services
Event Manager _____
Kitchen _____
Set Up _____
Waitstaff _____   Serving Style _____
Bar Service _____   Serving Style _____
Hors D'Oeuvres _____   Serving Style _____
Meal _____   Serving Style _____
Dessert _____   Serving Style _____
Miscellaneous _____
Subcontractors *(see attached)* _____
Clean Up _____
Overtime _____

The above is based on our agreed event plan attached. Any client additions or changes at the event or 24 hour preceding may be billed at time and a half.

Event sub-total $_____
Gratuities $_____
Tax $_____   *(if applicable)*
Total $_____
Deposit $_____   Due on _____
Balance $_____   Due on _____

Please sign this agreement and return with the deposit. Thank you.

For Hampton Catering_____   Date_____
Client _____   Date_____

Hampton Caterers

222 Ocean Street / Metropolis, USA 10011
Phone   123-456-7890   Fax   123-456-7890

NEW ACCOUNT CREDIT FORM

Client _____   Owner _____
Address _____   Buyer _____
_____   Telephone _____
Type of Business _____   Year Established _____
_____
Referred by _____

Credit References

Bank _____
_____
_____
Account # _____
Telephone _____   Contact _____

Business References

1 _____
  _____
2 _____
  _____
3 _____
  _____
  _____

Comments

Hampton Caterers

222 Ocean Street / Metropolis, USA 10011
Phone   123-456-7890   Fax   123-456-7890

EVENT PLAN

Date _____   Invoice # _____

Client _____   Client File # _____

Billing Address _____   Telephone—Day _____

_____   Telephone—Night _____

Host _____   Event _____

Location _____   Date of Event _____

_____   Time of Event _____

Hampton Coordinator _____   Type of Function _____

65

Hampton Caterers

222 Ocean Street / Metropolis, USA 10011
Phone   123-456-7890   Fax   123-456-7890

MENU

Date _____   Invoice # _____
Client _____   Client File # _____
Billing Address _____   Telephone—Day _____
_____   Telephone—Night _____
Host _____   Event _____
Location _____   Date of Event _____
_____   Time of Event _____
Hampton Coordinator_____   Type of Function _____

Wedding Reception

Assorted Hot and Cold Hors d'Oeuvres

Miniature Rolls

Whole Poached Salmon

Sauce Mousseline

Cucumber-Dill Dressing

Fresh Fruit Salad on Bed of Mesclun

Crisp Duck à l'Orange

Wild Rice with Mushrooms

Asparagus Drizzled with Cream

Strawberries and Whipped Cream

Wedding Cake with Edible Gold Leaf and Flowers

Chocolate Champagne Truffles

Coffee   Tea

Open Bar

Mineral Water

Poured White and Red Wine

Champagne Toast

Notes:

Hampton Caterers

222 Ocean Street / Metropolis, USA 10011
Phone   123-456-7890   Fax   123-456-7890

MENU—with instructions for wait staff

Date _____	Invoice # _____
Client _____	Client File # _____
Billing Address _____	Telephone—Day _____
_____	Telephone—Night _____
Host _____	Event _____
Location _____	Date of Event _____
_____	Time of Event _____
Hampton Coordinator _____	Type of Function _____

Waitperson name

Maitre d'

Dress

Meeting place

Arrival time

Staff meal provided

Meal time

Probable overtime

Type of service course by course

Location of stations

Special Meals

Hampton Caterers

222 Ocean Street / Metropolis, USA 10011

Phone   123-456-7890   Fax   123-456-7890

KITCHEN MENU—attach to shopping list and recipes for kitchen file

Date _____   Invoice # _____

Client _____   Client File # _____

Billing Address _____   Telephone—Day_____

_____   Telephone—Night _____

Host _____   Event _____

Location _____   Date of Event _____

_____   Time of Event _____

Hampton Coordinator_____   Type of Function _____

Hampton Caterers

222 Ocean Street / Metropolis, USA 10011
Phone   123-456-7890   Fax   123-456-7890

MENU—BEVERAGE PLAN

Date _____ Invoice # _____

Client _____ Client File # _____

Billing Address _____ Telephone—Day_____

_____ Telephone—Night _____

Host _____ Event _____

Location _____ Date of Event _____

_____ Time of Event _____

Hampton Coordinator_____ Type of Function _____

Menu Approved by_____

Ingredients to be in commissary by (date) _____

Chef _____

Beverage controller_____

Are special liquor licenses required? _____

Wine and liquor provided by_____

Delivered to_____

Delivered by (date) _____

Set-ups provided by _____

Ice;   Delivered___   Available on premises___   Storage needed___   Available___

Bartender(s) _____

Water?___   Bottled?___   Available on premises?___

Coffee

House Blend___   Espresso___   Cappucino___   Decaf___   Other___

Special equipment needed _____

Refrigeration for milk needed _____

Type of service _____

Tea

Orange pekoe___   Assorted Herbals___   Other___

Cups and saucers required

Demi tasse cups and saucers required

Glassware and stemware required

On Premises

From Commissary

From Rental

Are there adequate wash-up for re-use facilities on premises

Hampton Caterers

222 Ocean Street / Metropolis, USA 10011
Phone 123-456-7890   Fax 123-456-7890

SUBCONTRACTORS

Date _____   Invoice # _____

Client _____   Client File # _____

Billing Address _____   Telephone—Day _____

_____   Telephone—Night _____

Host _____   Event _____

Location _____   Date of Event _____

_____   Time of Event _____

Hampton Coordinator_____   Type of Function _____

Hampton Caterers

222 Ocean Street / Metropolis, USA 10011
Phone   123-456-7890   Fax   123-456-7890

IN-HOUSE KITCHEN PLAN

Date _____   Invoice # _____

Client _____   Client File # _____

Billing Address _____   Telephone—Day _____

_____   Telephone—Night _____

Host _____   Event _____

Location _____   Date of Event _____

_____   Time of Event _____

Hampton Coordinator _____   Type of Function _____

Hampton Caterers

222 Ocean Street / Metropolis, USA 10011
Phone   123-456-7890   Fax   123-456-7890

IN-HOUSE SERVICE PLAN

Date _____   Invoice # _____

Client _____   Client File # _____

Billing Address _____   Telephone—Day _____

_____   Telephone—Night _____

Host _____   Event _____

Location _____   Date of Event _____

_____   Time of Event _____

Hampton Coordinator _____   Type of Function _____

ℋampton Caterers

222 Ocean Street / Metropolis, USA 10011

Phone   123-456-7890   Fax   123-456-7890

FUNCTION SHEET

Date _____   Invoice # _____

Client _____   Client File # _____

Billing Address _____   Telephone—Day_____

_____   Telephone—Night _____

Host _____   Event _____

Location _____   Date of Event _____

_____   Time of Event _____

Hampton Coordinator_____   Type of Function _____

In charge site inspector
in charge commissary kitchen staff
in charge location kitchen staff
in charge liquor staff (are licenses in order, ice, on premises, storage)
packing
delivery driver
in charge set up staff
in charge subcontractors
valet parking
coatroom
lounges
other

service
Maitre d'
staff
bar
busing
sanitation
clean up
pack up to leave
return driver

ℋampton Caterers

222 Ocean Street / Metropolis, usa 10011
Phone   123-456-7890   Fax   123-456-7890

EQUIPMENT NEEDED

Date _____   Invoice # _____

Client _____   Client File # _____

Billing Address _____   Telephone—Day _____

_____   Telephone—Night _____

Host _____   Event _____

Location _____   Date of Event _____

_____   Time of Event _____

Hampton Coordinator _____   Type of Function _____

Item	From Hampton commissary	Available on premises	Other

Hampton Caterers

222 Ocean Street / Metropolis, USA 10011
Phone 123-456-7890   Fax 123-456-7890

SUBCONTRACTORS

Date _____   Invoice # _____
Client _____   Client File # _____
Billing Address _____   Telephone—Day_____
_____   Telephone—Night_____
Host _____   Event _____
Location _____   Date of Event _____
_____   Time of Event _____
Hampton Coordinator_____   Type of Function _____

Florist *(see attached)*
Bouquets
Boutonnieres
Centerpieces
Aisle
Altar
Tent
Wall
Column
Plants
· Other
Platter Garnish

Photographer *(see attached)*
Pre-event
event

Music *(see attached)*
Band
Singer
Pianist
Instruments
DJ
Sound System
Other
Please note arrangements for meals and mealtimes

Entertainment *(see attached)*
Emcee
Speaker
Magician
Performers
Fireworks
Other
Please note arrangements for meals and mealtimes

75

Hampton Caterers

222 Ocean Street / Metropolis, USA 10011
Phone   123-456-7890   Fax   123-456-7890

PREMISES

Date _____   Invoice # _____

Client _____   Client File # _____

Billing Address _____   Telephone—Day _____

_____   Telephone—Night _____

Host _____   Event _____

Location _____   Date of Event _____

_____   Time of Event _____

Hampton Coordinator _____   Type of Function _____

Apartment
Private house
Private garden
Public park
Hall
Chapel
Room
Tent
Historical Site
Botanical Garden

Requirements:
wheelchair access to all rooms and lounges

parking

SITE CHECK

Equipment (2 tents, 1 floor, lights, no heaters needed, small dance floor,) heavy duty extension cords, outdoor lights, speakers, microphone, piano, tables and chairs.

Sample Rental List (Partial)

CHAIRS:

All Wood folding chair (camp) ....
Armchair ....
Armchair—Tablet Folding, School
  type ....
Baby booster chair ....
Bar stools ....
Black fabric padded folding chair
  deluxe gold metal frame ....
Black plastic folding chair, plastic
  seat and back, Metal frame ....
Black Reception chairs ....
Black wood frame, black padded seat
Blue upholstered folding chair,
  deluxe, Gold metal frame, padded
  seat and back ....
Brown fabric upholstered deluxe,
  Gold metal padded seat & back....
Children's chairs, 13″ high with back
Gold fabric upholstered folding
  Chairs, deluxe Gold metal frame
  foam rubber, padded seat &
Gold metal frame, Gold velour
  seat and back ....
Green upholstered folding chair,
  deluxe, Gold metal frame, foam
  rubber, padded seat and back ....
High Chairs ....
Reception chair, non-folding,
  spindle back Gold Frame, Green,
  Red, Gold or Black seats ....
Red fabric upholstered folding chair,
  foam rubber seat and back, Gold
  metal frame ....

TABLES:

Walnut Formica snack table ....
Super Bridge—30″ × 30″ ....
Banquet:
  4 ft × 30 in. wide—Seats 4 to 6..
  6 ft. × 30 in. wide—Seats
  8 to 10 ....
  8 ft. × 30 in. wide—Seats
  10 to 12 ....
Round Cocktail Tables, 24 in.
  Pedestal type base
30 in. Pedestal type base ....
  Round 36″, Seats 4 (Bridge type) .
  Round 39″, Seats 5 ....
Round 42″, Seats 6 ....
Found 48″, Seats 8 ....
Round 54″, Seats 8 to 10 ....
Round 60″, Seats 10 ....
Round 72″, Seats 12 ....
Oval, 5 ft × 36 in. wide, Seats 8 ..
Oval, 6 ft. × 36 in. wide, Seats 10 ..
Oval, 6 ft. × 48 in. wide, Seats 12 ..
Oval, 7-1/2 ft. × 54 in. wide, Seats
  14 ....
Special, 4 ft. × 24 in. wide ....
  6 ft × 18 in. wide ....
  6 ft. × 24 in. wide ....
  8 ft. × 24 in. wide ....

SPECIAL DISPLAY TABLES:

1/4 Round Sections, 4 sections make
  10 ft. round table with cut out in
  center ....
1/2 60″ Round Table for display .....
Risers: 4 ft. × 12 in. × 12 in. ....
Risers: 5 ft. × 12 in. × 12 in. ....
6 ft. Formica top table ....
8 ft. Formica top table ....
Set of rubber Wheels for any table ...

BARS:

2-1/2 ft. Bar ....
4 ft. Bar ....
6 ft. Bar ....
Deluxe Rolling Bar ....
Bar Rubber Mat ....
Bar Stools ....
Wine Steward's Key on gold-plated
  chain ....
Cocktail Shaker, stainless steel,
  complete ....

DANCE FLOORS—INDOOR:

Rola-Flor, 10 ft. × 10 ft. ....
Rola-Flor, 10 ft. × 20 ft. ....
3′ × 3′ parquet sections................
Bandstands, runways, speakers'
  platforms, dance (tent and
  canopies to order) ....

CHINAWARE:

Dinner Plate, Cake and Salad
  Plate, Bread and 1 Deep Dish
  Dessert, Cup, Saucer, Demi
  Cup and Saucer, Bouillon Cup,
  Soup Plate
Gold Band ....
Silver Band ....
White China, swirl edge (limited
  qty.) ....
Black octagon ....
Masterpiece translucent china, all
  white ....
Platinum rim with floral design
  (limited qty.) ....
Kosher, new china ....
Ginon thin scalloped gold band
  (limited qty.) ....
French Imported Glass dishes / (may
  be used for Kosher) ....
Tea & Toast Sets—China ....
China Bowl—Extra Large ....
China Platters 16″ ....
China Platter—Extra Large ....
China Gravy Boats ....
Tea & Toast—Glass......................

GLASSWARE:

Hi-Ball Whiskey (shot) Glasses,
  Juice, Old Fashioned Fruit
  Sherbet ....
Punch Cups, Ash Trays ....
Old-Fashioned Beer Mugs, Parfait,
  Iced Tea Glasses ....
Coffee Mugs, white milk glass or
  white china ....
Double Old-Fashioned or Double
  High Ball ....
Glass Pitcher ....
Fruit Supreme ....
Glass Ice Bowl ....
Glass Ice Bowl, Large ....
Nappies ....
Nappy underliner........................

STEMWARE:

Pony, Brandy Snifter, Liqueur,
  Cordial ....
Cocktail, Whiskey Sour, Wine,
  Manhattan or Stemmed Sherbet ....
Champagne, Water Goblets ....
8 or 10 oz. Continental Wine or
  Irish Coffee ....
Solid Stem Imported Stemware,
  Queen Mary Imported Design ....
French Imported Crystal ....
Jumbo Wine Goblet, 17-1/2 oz. ....
Tulip Grande Wine......................
All Purpose Stem Goblet ....
Tulip Champagne ....
Flute Champagne—Crystal ....

SILVERWARE:

Knife, Dinner Fork, Salad Fork or
  Cake Fork, Teaspoon, Oyster
  Fork, Butter Spreader, Demi-
  Spoon, Iced Tea Spoon, Soup
  Spoon ....
Rogers Silverplate (American Lady) .
King George Silverplate.................
Deluxe Silverplate, Chalfonte (for
  formal dining) (limited qty.) ....
Stainless Steel........................
Silverplate Serving Spoons or Cold
  Meat Fork ....
Cake Server ....
Kosher (New Silverware)...............
Gold Flatware ....
Gold Serving Spoon or Fork ....
S/S Serving Spoon or Fork ....
Bowls, Revere:
  5″ ....
  7″ ....
  10″ ....
  12″ ....
Bread Tray, Silver ....
Bud Vase, Silver ....
Butter Dishes, Silver ....
Cake Knife ....
Cake Server, Silver ....
Cake Stand, 13 in. round 8 in. high .
Cake Stand, 2 tier, 2 Separate.........
Cake Stand, 3 tier, 3 Separate
  graduating stands ....
Candy Shells, Silver ....
Carving Knives ....
Carving Sets, Knife, Fork ....
Casserole—Electric ....
Cheese Knives ....
Cigarette Urn, Silver ....
Champagne Bucket, Silver ....
Champagne Stand with Wine
  Cooler, Silver ....
Coffee Server, Silver ....
Coffee Server, Silver Deluxe ....
Cookie Stand (Compots), Medium...
Finger Bowl with Liner, Silver ....
Fish Knife or Cheese Knife
  (Individual) ....
French Servers ....
Fruit Bowl, Oval, Silver ....
Fruit Knife, Silver ....
Gravy Boats, Silver with underliners .
Gravy Ladle, Silver ....
Gravy Boat, underliner, Silver ....
Ice Bucket with Cover ....
Ice Tongs ....
Ice Buckets, Plain, Silver ....
Lazy Susan, 3 Tier tid-bit dish type ..
Lazy Susan, 5 compartments—flat
  revolving, 18″ diameter, 3″ high ...
Lemon Trays, Silver ....
Mint Stand, Small, Silver ....
Mint Stand, Large, Silver...............
Nappy Dish with Liner, Silver
  (quantity limited).....................
Punch Cups, Silver ....
Party Scale, Silver ....
Relish Dishes, Olive, Celery, Pickle ..
Salad Dressing, 3 Dip ....
Salt & Pepper Shakers, Silver.........
Silent Butler, Silver ....
Server, Oval Glass Liner ....
Soup Ladle, Silver......................
Soup Tureens with Ladle and
  underliner ....
Spoon or Fork, Serving ....
Serving Spoon or Fork, Long
  Handled, Deluxe ....
Sugar Tongs ....
Sugar & Creamer, Silver ....
  Tray for above, Silver ....
Tea Kettle, Swinging, Silver ....
Vegetable Dish, 2 Compartments .....
Water Pitchers, Silver..................
Wine Cooler and Stand (Chrome) ....
Wine Cooler—Top Part of Above
  (Chrome) ....
Wine Cooler, Silver—Top Part of
  Champagne Stand ....

CHAFING DISHES:

Silverplate, Canned Heat
2 qt. round..................
2 qt. Deluxe 2 comp. sc ....
3 qt. rd. deluxe chafer with pyrex
liner ....
Extra liner for 3 qt. chafer...........
3 qt. square chafer......................
Twin Silver chafer, each pan 2 qt ..
1 gal. round ....
6 qt. round deluxe......................
7 qt. round deluxe.......................
Oval Chafer, Alcohol Heat ....
Stainless Steel, Canned Heat
1 gal. oblong—1 compartment .....
2 gal. oblong—1 compartment .....
2 gal. oblong—2 compartments....
2 gal. oblong—3 compartments....
1 gal. oblong—1
compartment—Electric.............
2 gal. oblong—1
compartment—Electric ....
Stainless Steel Marmite Dish............
Extra Food Pan for Chafing Dishes ..
Extra Water Pans ....
Crepe Suzette Pans ....
Recharge Lamps ....
Food Warming Lights ....
Fondue Sets...................................
Extra cans Canned Heat ....

SERVING PIECES, CHINA & GLASS:

Ash Trays, Glass ....
Ash Trays, China ....
Bud Vase, Glass ....
Bud Vase, Crystal ....
Carafe ....
Candlestick, Glass ....
Celery Dish, Glass...........................
Fish Platter, Glass, Small ....
Fish Platter, Glass, Large ....
Oil & Vinegar Service (Cruet).........
Gravy Boats, China...........................
Ice Bowls, Glass..............................
Olive Dish, Glass ....
Platters, China ....
Relish Dish, Glass............................
Salad Bowl, China ....
Salad Bowl, Glass, Large ....
Salad Bowl, Silver Rim....................
Salad Bowl, Large Glass French
Crystal..
Salad Bowl, Plastic, Individual.........
Salt & Pepper, China......................
Salt & Pepper, Glass ....
Salt & Pepper, Crystal ....
Shrimp Server, Glass, Silver Liner ...
Sugar & Creamer, China ....
Sugar & Creamer, Cut Crystal Style .
Sugar & Creamer, Glass...................
Vegetable Bowl, 2 comp. China ......
Vegetable Bowls, China....................
Water Pitcher, Glass ....
Water Pitcher, Crystal.....................

COFFEE POTS:

7-Piece Silver Deluxe Coffee and
Tea Set—Tea Pot, Coffee Pot,
Sugar, Creamer, Waste Bowl
Tray, Deluxe Urn—30 Cup ....
5-Piece Silver Tea and Coffee
Service—Coffee Pot, Tea Pot,
Sugar, Creamer and Tray ....
Coffee Makers—
Percolator, Electric, 30 Cup ....
Percolator, Electric, 48 Cup ....
?????, 55 Cup Stainless Steel
Deluxe................................

PUNCH SETS & FOUNTAINS:

Punch Set—Silver Deluxe—
Consisting of Bowl on Pedestal,
Long-Handled Ladle, and 12
Silver Punch Cups on Silver
Tray ....
Punch Bowl, Silver, Ladle, 3 gal.
No Cups ....
Punch Bowl, Silver, Ladle, 5 gal.
No Cups ....
Punch Sets, Glass Bowls, Silver
Ladle and 12 Glass Cups—2-1/2
gallon Bowl..................................
Punch Sets, Crystal Bowl, Silver
Ladle and 12 Glass Cups...............
Punch Fountain, electric, 3 gal. ....
Punch Fountain, electric, 5 gal. ....
Punch Ladle, Silver...........................
Punch Cups, Glass (extra).................
Punch Cups, Silver (extra) ....
Base for Glass Bowl........................

S I X

The Staff

In the catering business it is essential to be able to know how to do it all. If you do not know how long it takes to clear one hundred settings, set up a champagne toast, pack up the commissary, and load the truck, it will be difficult to know what to expect from the people working with you. It is easy to underestimate the actual time it takes to get a job done. Caterers often work under pressure of time in makeshift conditions, so compatibility as well as experience and stability is part of the job description.

From the start you will have one or more full- or part-time employees. Under current rules, anyone you are paying $50 or more a month would almost certainly be classified as an employee and must be treated under IRS considerations. If you call the IRS, you will eventually reach a representative who will tailor an information packet to your needs. For example, IRS Publication 15-Circular E will define who is an employee. They also have guidelines on self-employment, independent contractor, and consultant tax requirements. It is always useful and mostly necessary to speak with your accountant about these things, but it is helpful to have some preparation for what to expect.

The law requires you to know whether people in your employ are citizens. You must see proof of residency or other papers that entitle them to work in the United States. The green card is one such document. You are also obliged to make sure you are in compliance with child labor laws. The youngest age for full-time employment in most states is sixteen unless special working papers are supplied. There are minimum wage and overtime rates for the food-service field that have to be honored. Disability and unemployment insurance are also details that are regulated. Attention to what may seem at first like many nuisances will save a lot of grief and money in the long run.

The IRS, the Department of Labor, and the Small Business Administration all will assist with information. Of course, your lawyer, accountant, and business consultant also are sources of advice on compliance in these areas.

Workers' Compensation is an insurance policy that virtuallly all states require, much the way auto insurance is mandatory. It is an insurance policy that you can get from a private carrier or from a special state agency acting like a carrier.

CATERER STAFFING

The *kitchen staff* may at first simply assist you or complement your skills. But if you yourself are not going to be the chef, your first hiring task will be a chef. Depending on the size of the job and your baking skills, you may choose to get breads, rolls, and pastries from an outside source. Hiring a good baker who will work on a part-time basis is an alternative. If you prefer not to bake, it is handy to have someone who will. Hiring a baker who is willing and able to prepare main dishes is, of course, another option. You do want someone who has had professional experience, so that you can look away occasionally.

The *wait staff*, and their value, cannot be overemphasized since the service is what can make or break an event. From the start, you have to treat the staff like the professionals they are. No matter how good the food is or how beautifully it is plated, if it is not served in a pleasing, expert way, the guests will not have a good time. Until you develop your own Rolodex, agencies, universities, and culinary schools are good sources.

When you are just starting, you may ask wait staff to help pack the food, pick up the rental items, and prep when you get to the location. They will probably arrange tables and chairs and set the tables too, to say nothing of cleaning up and returning everything. Some of the people you hire may work twelve hours straight, so it is important to discuss overtime not only with your client but with the staff as well.

Barpersons, people who know not only about wine and liquor but serving portions and the appropriate law, have the right and the obligation to refuse to serve a minor or someone who has obviously had too much to drink. Under almost all circumstances where a guest has had one drink too many, the barperson should speak with the party manager, or in their absence, the host, and tactfully but firmly tell them that a guest needs transportation home. There are reported cases in many states where the bartender and the bar owner have been found liable for injuries resulting from a drunk driver.

Production assistants do food ordering and shopping, stocking and inventory, prepping and packing. Choose someone energetic, intelligent, and beginning a foodservice career.

The *office team* includes a part-time bookkeeper to make sure client bills go out and bills and taxes are paid. When your business takes off, you might want the pleasure and luxury of someone full-time to handle correspondence, work charts, orders, and some phone work so that you can come and go as freely as you need to. It is important that when someone other than yourself answers the phone it is with the same inviting warmth you would use. Client contact comes first.

Buspersons not only clear tables and fill coffee cups, but help replace serving dishes, coffee urns and so forth if it is too large a party for the wait staff to do.

The *cleaning staff* hold essential positions which must be filled with as much care and respect as any other because your business license depends on it. Everything has to be cleaned all the time, not just pots, dishes, and appliances, but walls and floors, bathrooms, even the office and vehicles are held to a higher standard than in other businesses because you handle food. It is also possible to hire the same people to do cleanup off-premise as well.

Drivers need to have commercial drivers licenses and be familiar with local rules and regulations. You might hire a driver and a vehicle, but then you must be sure the van is used for food only because it must be clean and free of chemical odors and other pollutants that would affect food. Is the driver doing only drop-off and pick-up, or are they part of the off-premise team? You are responsible, so the driver must inform you of any maintenance or repairs that are necessary.

When you want to expand your business you may want the services of a part-time *sales person*. Choose someone who has had experience selling foodservices and can reflect your particular abilities and product to represent you to potential clients. They should also reflect your own sense of social etiquette and interpersonal skills.

A *party manager or account coordinator* is an asset when your business grows, or at a busy season like the month of June, when there are frequently weddings and graduation parties. The manager is the person you will introduce your client to after the event has been committed. He or she will be the liaison person for all questions the client has, from the color of the linens to the size of the plates, the photographers to the location and menu. The manager will create work schedules, determine the staff needed, and field any problems. The party manager will make sure everyone is on time and may be the one to go to the location for the duration of the event. The party coordinator may get a fixed percent of the income from an event that they have been in charge of.

Your own management skills will grow as you need them. Offer competitive wages, gratuities, and pleasant working conditions and you more than compensate for lack of experience as an employer. Communicate clearly about tasks, breaks, and meals, and never be too busy to listen. Rehire the part-time and independent people you enjoy working with because it establishes a positive working relationship that builds confidence.

In catering—especially in a new and small business—people have to be flexible about tasks. A buser may also be the parking valet, and wait staff may help take coats. Everyone helps to pack up and leave the premises. Your pre-event function sheet will spell this out and each employee should receive a schedule of what his or her duties are before the start of each function.

General safety rules have to be in effect at all times to prevent accidents and all employees should know where the first-aid kit is as well as the fire extinguisher.

Perks can often be spelled out like transportation, parking, meals, and leftovers. Most of the time, gratuities are simply added to the bill and divided among the staff. Many places have a policy of individual gratuities being pooled and shared as well.

Dress codes are important. Nothing and no one can be clean enough. Even the illusion of dirt worries people. In addition to food sanitation, which is very specific, everyone working has to be sure their persons and clothes are very clean. Tuxedos, black and white, or a color and white classic clothes are the standard attire for servers. The traditional kitchen whites, abundant aprons, side towels for food preparers, and skirts or pants are, of course, variables depending often on regional tastes. There is certainly no need to be rigid about wardrobe, but staff should be pleasantly and identifiably dressed.

A minimum of the most simple jewelry is okay, but heavy stuff or anything dangling is dangerous and it gets very hot when you reach into an oven or stand over a steam table. There is nothing to be done about guests who wear scents that overpower food aromas, but staff really should never have more than a touch.

Generally, kitchen staff is provided whites when they are prepping and cooking off-premise and wait and bar staffs supply their own, but there are no fixed rules.

There are a few *nos*, such as no smoking, gum chewing, drinking, lateness, contagious illness, open cuts or sores or colds. And no long chats with the guests, although most events are not so formal that pleasantries are not exchanged. Even among themselves, staff should keep public conversations brief, so that the guests feel they are the ones getting the attention.

In any task-oriented situation the goal is to find mutually beneficial solutions, to delegate work, and to maintain customer satisfaction. Accurate information and clear intentions will prevent most conflicts. If you perceive performance problems, it is your responsibility to address them and assess the facts and feelings of the matter at hand. Developing techniques of self-discipline and managing conflict will emerge as you coordinate everyone's contributions. Frequently, you will insist and occasionally accommodate. Communication, commitment, and a little compromise go a long way. The buck stops with you, and sometimes listening to complaints and constructive criticism comes with the territory.

There is a show-time element, so roles have to be assigned meticulously and performed punctually and graciously. Clearly, the staff has to be supportive of each other, collegial rather than competitive. By the same token, your staff should never have to put up with embarrassment or abuse. You or the event manager will have to be the diplomat and handle a negative situation in support of anyone working for you.

STAFF DIRECTORY

Small Business Administration
Management Aids
P.O. Box 15434
Fort Worth, TX 76119
Phone: (800) 827-5722

Department of Labor
Office of Information
201 Varick Street
New York, NY 10014
Phone: (212) 337-2319

Child Labor Information
Phone: (212) 264-8185

Minimum Wage and Overtime
Phone: (212) 264-8185

United States Government Department of Treasury
IRS
Tax Information
Phone: (800) 829-1040
Tax Forms
Phone: (800) 829-3676

Workers' Compensation Board
Public Information Office
180 Livingston Street
Brooklyn, NY 11248
Phone: (718) 802-6651

Local Telephone Directory
(Department of Labor)
(Workers' Compensation Board)

SEVEN

The Premises

One of the delights of catering is that in addition to hotels and reception halls, any site is a possible location. Not only private homes and gardens, but parks, museums, historical mansions, corporate headquarters, ballparks, renovated train stations, and even trains and boats. Abandoned mines, bridges, rooftops, and schoolyards all can serve, morning, noon, or night as alternatives for caterers. Catering is done on movie sets, opera stages, in airplane hangars, public libraries, and town halls.

Most large events done by start-up caterers are basically stand-up, whether there are tables and chairs for the guests or not. Since service is circumscribed, it is the setting that will create the environment for pleasure that all partygivers and partygoers expect.

The design of the premises is often the caterer's job and the ambience will be the first impression the guests get of an event. Food presentation must be inviting at each station. Your food standards must be reflected in the quality of the ambience you instill. It is not a substitute for delicious food in the proper amount, but it enhances anything served.

Style is personal, but in catering it has to be a consensus. Your client does not want to walk into an event they are hosting and wonder where they are. If it is a very large party, it is best for you to have a few samples of colors and a few sketches or photographs. (These can be gleaned from magazines until you develop your own photo file.) Refer to them in your confirmation letter and, if possible, have a floor plan or sketch of the arrangement you have in mind.

The atmosphere contributes greatly to how much enjoyment people have. One or two unique touches are usually enough. Mainly the task is to harmonize the occasion, setting, and food. Decor can be selected either to turn a neutral space into a specific theme or one that fits in with the surroundings.

If you are not familiar with the site, do not make any assumptions. Check it out first. There are sometimes features over which you will have no control. Though you will not have a backup location, you will be able to have backup equipment. Portable equipment and decor can be delivered almost anywhere, for a price. If there is a potential difficulty for a complicated event, make sure someone is in charge of the equipment. They will confirm delivery, make sure it is operational on location, and supervise its maintenance and return. The commissary must be functional at all times and geared up for special events to coordinate with the event location. Catering is a one-opportunity occasion, so a missed detail has a ripple effect.

The account manager goes to the site of the selected location and walks through the facility, sometimes with a Polaroid camera and tape measure, making notes and making sure what will actually be there. It is also necessary to find out when the area will be free to set up and the time you must have everything out. In addition to the party area, kitchen, washroom, coatroom, and social area, questions about smoke detectors, fire exits, emergency lights, insurance and security, access, parking, zoning, permits, and liabilities must be answered. Is there wheelchair access to both dining area and washrooms? Are elevators usable at all times?

Off-premise catering is an exercise in creative hospitality. Your client is expecting a high level of pleasure which the caterer has to build with nuts and bolts, like organizing supply and waste management routines and delegating on-site tasks to reliable people. Performance-oriented schedules will lead to very productive relationships with staff and subcontractors.

The technical aspects are the same serving a New Mexican menu or northern Italian specialties. Whether the theme is ultramodern, nostalgic, personal, public, relaxed to formal, tent to ballroom, food must be delivered, prepared, served, and removed. Clean dishes have to be plated and dirty ones washed. The person in charge and a second emergency person must be listed so that the premises are accessible the day of the event and the day after.

Directions to the premises must be clear and parking available. If there is not an easily accessed parking lot, there are insured valet parking services that supply bonded uniformed personnel to parties. They will do everything related to parking that a large event requires. Since they give the first and last impression of service, capable professional service is important. Valet services often know who to call about police permits and have good rapport with people who handle traffic. It is well worth hiring them as they will accept all liability and understand various conditions that prevail in both urban and suburban locations. They will look at the site and determine the best way to handle it.

LOCATION DIRECTORY

Barns of Wolf Trap
    1635 Trap Road
    Vienna, VA
    Phone: (703) 938-8463

Belmont Mansion
    Fairmont Park
    Philadelphia, PA 19131
    Phone: (215) 878-8844

Biltmore Estate
    One Biltmore Plaza
    Asheville, NC 28803
    Phone: (704) 274-1776

Brooklyn Botanical Garden
    1000 Washington Street
    Brooklyn, NY 11225
    Phone: (718) 622-4433

Hampton National Historic Site
535 Hampton Lane
Towson, MD 21204
Phone: (301) 823-7054

Ladew Topiary Gardens
3535 Jarrettsville Pike
Monkton, MD 21111
Phone: (410) 557-9570

Lincoln Park
2200 North Canon Drive
Great Hall of Cafe Brauer
Chicago, IL 60614
Phone: (312) 280-2767
(Indoor and outdoor available)

LOCAL PHONEBOOK LISTINGS
Arboretum
Botanic Garden
Chamber of Commerce
Convention and Visitors Center
Cultural Councils
Landmark Commission
National Historic Sites
Parks Department
Yacht Clubs and Marinas

Los Angeles County Arboretum
301 North Baldwin Avenue
Arcadia, CA 91006
Phone: (818) 821-3211

National Museum of Women in the Arts
1250 New York Avenue, N.W.
Washington, DC 20005
Phone: (202) 783-5000

The Nature Conservancy
Phone: (800) 628-6860
(Will provide information about sites from pine barrens, prairies, bird preserves, and riverbanks to waterfalls, savannahs, and seashores that permit and have the capacity to accommodate special events.)

New York Botanical Gardens
Southern Boulevard and 200 Street
Bronx, NY 10458
Phone: (718) 220-8700

Old Town Hall
3999 University
Fairfax, VA 22030
Phone: (703) 385-7976

Point Defiance
Tacoma, WA
Phone (206) 305-1000

The Daybreak Star Indian Cultural Center
Discovery Park
Seattle, WA 98199
Phone: (206) 285-4425

U.S. National Arboretum
3501 New York Avenue, N.E.
Washington, DC 20002
Phone: (202) 399-5958

Union Station
The Columbus Club
50 Massachusetts Avenue, N.E.
Washington, DC 20002
Phone: (202) 289-8300

Advanced Parking Concepts, Inc.
309 Bloomfield Avenue
Verona, NJ 07044
Phone: (201) 857-2008

EIGHT

Nonfood Supplies

A restaurant, once outfitted, is more or less a done deal, but caterers regularly encounter situations quite different from previous ones and have to set up and oversee an event in an environment over which they have little control. While the possibilities to be creative are endless, the means are not. Because of the higher impact of any glitches, the quality or performance of nonfood supplies can make or break a party.

What is trendy is easy. A few accent pieces and colors will set a mood. Presentation platters, flowers, lights, and what is generally called ambience have to be gracious but not so pretentious they makes people uncomfortable. Commodious tables and comfortable, affordable chairs are always welcome.

Outside suppliers are your best tool. Local rental companies will provide tables, chairs, and linens. Don't forget satellite tables for people to set down dishes or glasses they are done with, as well as one for gifts or presentations as the occasion warrants. The off-premise kitchen, however makeshift, must also have adequate prep and plating tables.

Restaurant-supply houses have commercial equipment: warmers; hot plates; chafing dishes; warming, convection, and microwave ovens; grills; and warming lamps as well as knives, sharpeners, and wooden cutting boards. Sometimes the caterer just brings the prepared food and it has only to be plated and served. Insulated food containers will keep food hot or cold.

If on-site cooking has to be done, you want special-use items, such as electric skillets or woks, rice cookers, steamers, deep fryers. Do make sure you have hand-lift cabinets for food and a dolly for heavy loads. Ice containers and tubs may be needed. If you have specialties like pizza, you might want some pizza stones and paddles. Pasta machines will be an asset for unique fresh flavors. Tea carts can be used for Spanish *tapas* and then for dessert. If the commissary is close to the event site, it might simply be more efficient to replenish the food fully prepared every hour or so.

It is a good idea to put together several site kits: a kitchen kit with a knife roll; sharpener; scissors; twine; bamboo skewers; funnels; scrapers; pot holders; pastry bag; cheesecloth; spoons; spatulas; tongs. A lemon zester and a juicer are handy also. Immersion blenders or hand mixers are useful as are stainless steel measuring cups, spoons, mixing bowls, colanders, and strainers. A few thermometers and timers as well as whisks, spatulas, and solid and slotted spoons should be organized so that they can do double duty off-premise. Pot holders, oven mitts, germicidal hand soap, detergent, extra aprons, and oversize towels can all go in a nylon duffle. Disposable products like aluminum foil, plastic wrap, paper towels, and tissues should be included. Also pack sealable heavy-duty garbage bags, and rubber gloves, both regular and heavy-duty (to deal with breakage, etc.). Ecologically correct disposables, such as paper instead of Styrofoam and biodegradable cleaning supplies are available.

Another useful site kit includes a first-aid kit and fire extinguisher, flashlight and batteries, heavy-duty extension cord, staple gun, gaffers tape, two-and three-pronged adapters, tape measure, level, pushpins, safety pins, needle and thread, hammer, nails, pliers, and Phillips and straight screwdrivers.

For packing, you might want bubble wrap, masking tape, clean, sturdy moving-company cartons, flexible foam, and heavy-duty shallow flexible food containers for leftovers. Hard ones crack and are best for light things like salads, cookies, or crackers, but very flexible ones are useless because they distort and break their seal. Collapsible plastic crates help carry last-minute things.

Virtually anything can be rented. Before you start purchasing, experience will teach what items are repeated the most for your clients' needs. For instance, rectangular covered chafing dishes, coffee urns, pitchers, and serving pieces for salads and bread in classically designed stainless will fit into almost any theme. Trays for hors d'oeuvres, serving, and busing and some stands for them are often used. Standard six-ounce stemmed goblets for wine and coordinated water glasses might be worth owning.

When you rent, it is best to work with a 10 percent overage, for guests who bring guests, to replace items dropped, for returns to the buffet, or for drinkers who switch drinks more than expected. For a large elaborate event, a more realistic figure is 25 percent over. It seems that the larger the party, the larger the percent of extra supplies are needed.

The rental company will provide lists and work with you from the start. Selections of first-course plate, soup plate, dinner plate, dessert plate, cup and saucer, and demitasse cup and saucer are readily available. For flatware, the selections are made from salad fork, dinner fork, dessert fork, butter knife, cutting knife, soup spoon, dessert spoon, coffee spoon, and demitasse spoon. Serving platters and bowls, salt shakers and pepper mills, condiment holders, sugar and creamers, utensils, and special items are equally obtainable. From punch bowls to barbecue grills, there are companies that will deliver on time for the function you are planning.

Purchases of disposable plastic and paper items are often necessary, so you might want to buy certain things like plastic luncheon or dinner plates in bulk. Oversized napkins and sturdy flatware will be used for events where the service costs need to be kept low. Paper doilies line trays and platters effectively and can also be bought by the case. Cardboard separators used between layers of large cakes are also handy for platters of tea sandwiches and other finger foods.

Linens are procured from the same house that rents the place settings. Beginning caterers usually rent all linens because each event is tabled and served differently for people with strong opinions about whether everything should be white, or a color, or combination of colors that never would have crossed your mind. It is also quite cost efficient, considering the cost of maintaining them in a pristine condition and matching replacements. Order generously sized napkins and enough cloths for dining and serving tables. Extra linens are a necessity, not a luxury. They cover spills and are needed under chafers and trays and for servers. For buffets, sometimes double the amount of napkins are rented because guests leave them about and reasonably will not pick up an unknown one. Renting is such an important part of catering that many large catering companies have actually expanded into the rental business. They are quite happy to rent to the competition and work in very collegial ways.

What to wear? Fashion in the culinary world exemplifies the adage that the more things change the more they remain the same. For the most part, good quality white chef's coats will get kitchen and food staffs through most events, and tuxedos are worn by wait staff at many traditional affairs.

Some men and women work in white linen casual jackets. Though white is so apparently clean, there are many situations where a uniformed look is inappropriate. When that is the case, discuss with your client whether simple white blouses or shirts and skirts or trousers will do. Safe and comfortable shoes are essential. For kitchen work, flexible clogs with rubber soles are almost universally liked, but there are many companies that make an informal dress shoe that is as safe as a pair of sneakers. The comfort level of your clients and their guests are your best advertisement and the wait staff needs to be easily identified so they can be approached without hesitation.

Tents are often the solution to events held in gardens, both public and private. The most basic tents will shelter from sun and rain. They can be as plain and elaborate as the budget permits. Floors and dance floors are easily arranged and heaters and lights can be installed. They should be professionally installed and taken down. Make sure that they are permitted on the grounds where the function is to take place. Runners and canopies can also be rented.

Caterers often function as consultants to their clients, and may be asked to hire and supervise florists, photographers, and musicians.

There are florists everywhere who will work to order and deliver the arrangements you want directly to the event. As with all subcontractors, it is good to establish a good relationship with a single florist after trying a few so that you can get the selections you want with some special care. If the client has a florist they want to use, there is no reason not to. Begin by asking hotels and restaurants with style you like who does their flowers. Simple decorative accents are not difficult to make and if you have a flair for it, an assortment of baskets with plastic liners and green florist's clay can be the basis for informal displays. If your area has flower markets or stalls, you can assemble refreshing arrangements at a good price. If kept in a cool place, they can be prepared up to twenty-four hours ahead of time. People have practiced by making gifts for friends and family. It is unlikely, though, that you will have time to take the flowers on. Check with floral designers, wholesalers, and florists to learn the best in your area. Plants and even trees can be rented. Garnish flowers for platters and buffet stations can be ordered anywhere, but edible flowers must come from a reliable source.

Displays and decorations have to be discussed in detail with the client, especially if it is a corporate or cultural function at which their taste is what they are trying to reflect. And they will have strong feelings about the environment to which they are inviting guests. From a boardroom lunch meeting to a picnic in the park, restraint and good taste are always in order.

Will the client supply the material and be responsible for setting it up? Will they want a theme decoration or a professional display? Special screening of films or videos are usually set up by the client if needed, but once again the yellow pages will provide you with even those resources.

Photographers are needed for many events and, by and large, you will find them through networking. You want to know what their product looks like before you commit them to your client's once-in-a-lifetime occasion. Do not hesitate to look at portfolios when you make your choice. Be certain you understand your client's specific needs and what they actually want to end up with. Photographs are very important to people and you cannot be too careful in your selection.

The same is true for musicians. Generally, the client makes the selection, but if you want to increase the services offered, you might listen to various groups, most of whom have tapes you can play for clients. It is also necessary to know if they have and will bring whatever instruments and electrical equipment they use. The size of the band is important as well. Some places just cannot handle more than four people and their instruments. Musicians and entertainers are also discoverable through colleges.

There are entertainers and supply houses that specialize in children's events and offer appropriate items. Most areas have companies that supply helium-filled balloons and deliver them. You can rent a helium tank from a resource in your area.

Licensed fireworks can be arranged. By and large, first-class fireworks are a thousand dollars a minute and not to be suggested lightly.

TAKING THE SHOW ON THE ROAD

For locations away from the commissary, in addition to the specific food and equipment for the event it is helpful to have several kits ready to go.

Office Kit—Briefcase

Petty cash
Emergency credit card
Copies of licenses, permits,
    contracts, and
    worksheets
Cellular telephone

On-site phone book
Business cards
Local map
Camera, extra film (regular
    and/or Polaroid)
Small flashlight

Emergency Site Kit—Large Metal Tool Chest

First-aid kit
Fire extinguisher
Fire extinguishing
 blanket
Two powerful
 flashlights
Extra batteries and
 bulbs
Hammer and nails
 (brads)
Phillips and regular
 screwdrivers

Needle and thread
Safety pins
Pushpins
Staple gun and
 staples
Matches
Gaffer's tape
Pliers
Tape measure
Metal polish &
 cloth

Heavy-duty rubber
 gloves
Heavy-duty
 garbage bags
Paper towels
Mat knife and
 blades
Metal straightedge
Steam iron
Heavy-duty
 extension cords

Two- and three-pronged electrical adapters

Kitchen Kit—Nylon Duffle Bag

Knife roll and
 knife sharpener
Twine
Bamboo skewers
Solid and slotted
 spoons
Solid and slotted
 spatulas
Long-handled fork
Lemon zester
Juice reamer
Stainless steel
 grater
Pot holders
Oven mitts
Portable radio
Measuring cups
Measuring spoons

Funnels
Whisks
Pastry bag
Tongs
Food
 thermometers
Can opener
Bottle opener
Corkscrew
Portable electric
 mixer
Cordless
 immersion
 blender
Assorted plastic
 bags and tubs

Germicidal hand
 soap
Detergent
Moisturizer
Extra aprons and
 towels
Rubber gloves
Sponges
Plastic wrap
Aluminum foil
Tissues
Matches
Plastic tarps
Masking tape
Grease pencil

NONFOOD PRODUCT DIRECTORY

AGA Stoves
17 Towne Farm Road
Stowe, VT 05672
Phone: (802) 253-9727

Artex International Linens
P.O. Box 309
Highland, IL 62249
Phone: (800) 851-8671; (618) 654-2113 /
    Fax: (618) 654-7672

Bragard Uniforms Inc,
215 Park Avenue South, Suite 705
New York, NY 10003
Phone: (212) 982-8031 / Fax: (212) 353-0318

Bridge Company
214 East 52 Street
New York, NY 10022
Phone: (212) 688-4220 (store)
Phone: (212) 838-6746 ($3 for catalog,
    deducted from first order)
(Kitchenware and more)

Chicago Cutlery
441 East Bonner Road
Wauconda, IL 60084
Phone: (708) 526-2144

Commercial Culinary
P.O. Box 7258
Arlington, VA 22207-0258
Phone: (800) 999-4949 / Fax: (703) 550-8034

CresCor Metal Products
12711 Taft Avenue
Cleveland, OH 44108
Phone: (216) 851-6800
(Insulated cabinets and dollies)

Frette Linens
    200 West 57 Street
    New York, NY 10019
    Phone: (800) 72-FRETTE; (212) 262-2740 /
        Fax: (212) 262-2740

FUSCO Fun Uniforms
    4104 24th Street, Suite 148
    San Francisco, CA 94114
    Phone: (800) 723-8726 (out of state); (800) 773-8726 (Calif.)

Garland Ranges
    111 West Chicago Avenue
    Hinsdale, IL 60521
    Phone: (708) 323-1011

Gourmet Gear Culinary Apparel
    233 Market Street, Suite C
    Venice, CA 90291
    Phone: (800) 682-4635; (310) 450-6698 /
        Fax: (310) 392-4657

Hilden Halifax Table Linens
    P.O. Box 1098
    South Boston, VA 24592
    Phone: (800) 431-2514 / Fax: (804) 572-4781

Hobart-Mixers
    Troy, OH 45374
    Phone: (513) 332-3000

Homer Laughlin China
    6th Street and Harrison
    Newell, WV 26050
    Phone: (800) 452-4462; (304) 387-1300 /
        Fax: (800) 533-8918; (304) 387-0593

iSi Siphons and cream whippers
    30 Chapin Road
    P.O. Box 616
    Pine Brook, NJ 07058
    Phone: (201) 227-2426 / Fax: (201) 227-9140

KitchenAid portable appliances
St. Joseph, MI 49085
Phone: (800) 422-1230

Lenox Hotelware China
100 Lenox Drive
Lawrenceville, NJ 08648
Phone: (609) 896-2800

Libbey Glass
P.O. Box 919
Toledo, OH 43693
Phone: (800) 824-1667; (419) 247-5000 /
Fax: (419) 727-2433

Magikitch'n
180 Penn Am Drive
Quakertown, PA 18951
Phone: (800) 441-1492
(Grills)

Maid of Scandinavia
3244 Raleigh Avenue
Minneapolis, MN 55416
Phone: (800) 328-6722
(Cake and decorating supplies and ingredients;
also packaging equipment)

Oneida Silversmiths, Foodservice Division
Oneida, NY 13421
Phone: (800) 258-1220 / Fax: (315) 361-3290

Sub-Zero Refrigeration
P.O. Box 4130
Madison, WI 53711
Phone: (608) 271-2233

Syracuse China Corporation
P.O. Box 4820
2900 Court Street
Syracuse, NY 13221
Phone: (800) 448-5711 / Fax: (315) 455-6763

Tents
Phone: (516) 694-TENT

Unic Espresso Machines
Silver Spoon Ltd.
12114 Nebel Street
Rockville, MD 20852
Phone: (301) 984-0970 / Fax: (301) 984-0973

Viking Stoves
111 Front Street
Greenwood, MS 38930
Phone: (601) 455-1200

Villeroy & Boch
41 Madison Avenue
New York, NY 10010
Phone: (800) 223-1762; (212) 683-1747 /
  Fax: (212) 481-0283

Volrath Kitchen Supplies
P.O. Box 611
Sheboygan, WI 53082-4851
Phone: (414) 457-4851 / Fax: (414) 459-6570
(Extensive catalog including catering specialties)

Vulcan-Hart Stoves
P.O. Box 696
Louisville, KY 40201
Phone: (800) 333-8021; (502) 778-2791 /
  Fax: (800) 333-1808

Williams-Sonoma Mail Order
P.O. Box 7456
San Francisco, CA 94120-7456
Phone: (800) 541-2233 / Fax: (415) 421-5153
(Equipment for cooking and dining)

Wilton Enterprises
2240 West 75 Street
Woodridge, IL 60517
Phone: (718) 963-7100
(Cake and decorating supplies and ingredients;
    also call for regional classes)

Wusthof Trident Cutlery
2 Westchester Plaza
Elmsford, NY 10523-054
Phone: (914) 347-2185

The "Restaurant Supply" section of your local yellow pages

NINE

Food Handling and Sanitation

According to New York State law, a caterer is a person who prepares and furnishes food at a commissary that is intended for individual portion service at the premises of the consumer, whether such premises are temporary or permanent. A caterer is considered a foodservice establishment operator and is required to perform in accordance with the statutes. A commissary is quite simply a place where food is stored, processed, and prepared. A copy of your state sanitary code is available and very helpful. Often the licensing requirements vary from county to county, and a good resource is your local board of health. You will probably need to take the twelve-to twenty-hour food protection training course offered by many schools and frequently by the field services of your local health department. If it is difficult to get to a school, you can even do it by mail. You or someone you work with will need a certificate stating you know the sanitation laws required to be in a foodservice business.

The basic guidelines have to do with cleanliness, but the specific routines of controlling bacteria and viruses have to be learned because it is critical that they are done right. Sometimes additional codes are amended and you will have to stay alert for them.

In New York State, for instance, it is now mandatory to refrigerate eggs between 35°F and 40°F. It has been discovered that even when the shell of an egg is not cracked, salmonella bacteria can multiply. Eggs stored properly will be fine for about one month. When cooking professionally, the best policy is to refrain from ever serving raw eggs, even in dishes like Caesar salad, mayonnaise, or eggnog. Eggs should be cooked within two hours of removal from refrigeration and served immediately after cooking. Egg-rich foods like custards, if refrigerated immediately, will keep for three to four days. When a recipe calls for cooking an egg mixture until it coats a metal spoon, it will have reached the 160°F necessary for thorough cooking. If you have any doubt, use a food thermometer. The United States Department of Agriculture (USDA) recommends that eggs, as well as meat, poultry, fish, and milk held at room temperature for more than two hours be discarded.

There are many places you can turn for up-to-the-minute information of food safety. The USDA Hot Line for Meat and Poultry is available 10:00 A.M. to 4:00 P.M. Eastern Time, Monday through Friday, and will answer specific questions about eggs as well. The Food and Nutrition Information Center of the USDA has a remarkable and diverse print and software library that is meticulously cataloged for your easy reference. They quite reasonably offer a disclaimer saying that inclusion in their files is not an endorsement by the USDA, nor do they insure the accuracy of all information. They have sections for foodservice management, nutrition and health education, food technology, and recipes. It is to your advantage to keep up with their listings because there are not enough hours in the day to seek out a full array of new information and run your business.

The Food and Nutrition Center, part of the National Agricultural Library located in Beltsville, Maryland, is also a treasure house of books, articles, and audiovisual material. They have an extensive research department that will help on a cost recovery basis, but a lot of basic and bibliographical information is available at no cost. They will also try to assist you with answering specific food and nutrition questions. The Food Safety and Inspection Service has catering-oriented newsletters and other pertinent information it will send on request.

Universities publish findings that are very helpful. Dr. Dean O. Cliver led the team from the Food Research Institute at the University of Wisconsin that proved wooden cutting boards are actually less of germ repositories and breeders than the plastic ones, given they are both cleaned equally well. Plastic retains germs under cleaning conditions that will destroy them on wooden cutting boards. Never let even the juices from raw meat, poultry, fish, or eggs touch any other food-preparation surface, utensil, or container. To avoid cross-contamination, wash not only the cutting board but the knife, fork, spatula, and countertops after use. Wash them with soap for twenty to thirty seconds and occasionally a mixture of one part chlorine bleach to fourteen parts hot water. Do not reuse marinades or pour them into anything that will be eaten uncooked like salads. Do not even think of cutting salad ingredients on a board you have just cut a chicken on without washing it thoroughly first. Never put grilled chicken or meat back onto the plate from which it was taken raw. Check instructions on the kitchenware and accessories for the appropriate cleaning agents to use. Baking soda solutions are still a good way to keep refrigerators free of mold.

The U.S. Government Printing Office will send a free catalog in which you will find a large number of booklets that are a wellspring of food and handling facts and guidelines. For a nominal cost you will be able to add them to your library. The American Frozen Food Institute is able to provide information in their area of expertise. All in all there is a fine network in place for guidance and support.

It may seem awkward at first to address the personal hygiene of the people whom you select to work with you, but you have no choice. Avoiding the issue can have a negative outcome. It would, for instance, appear obvious that if anyone is ill, they should not be handling food, but the sad truth is that when people have personal and professional obligations they often overlook the obvious. You cannot permit anyone with even a cold to handle food for very real reasons. As a matter of fact, anyone dealing with food publicly cannot even appear to be ill because it reduces confidence. In the catering business you are responsible for your clients' comfort level, and their happy event is not the time to educate them on the difference between what is contagious and what isn't. Food handlers have to wash their hands constantly, and stay home with even a slight cold. Though viruses and bacteria can be carried by air, water, food, pests, and dirty equipment, the most common means of transmission are the hands.

Hair, clothing, and shoes, of course, have to be clean and kitchen towels changed frequently. Whether you use uniforms like chef's jackets, casual wear, or unique expressions of personal style, everything must be immaculate and neat. Shoes should be comfortable, safe, and well-maintained. This is true if you are just delivering the food and neither setting it up nor serving it.

The best and often the only way to deal with food contamination is to prevent it. There really is no cure and the saying, "When in doubt throw it out," never had more meaning. You can keep grains, cereals, sugar, flour, dried beans, peas, and fruits at room temperature. Sugar and salt, herbs, spices, oils and vinegars, honey, and preserves and jams don't need refrigeration either. They do have to be stored in a clean, dry place free of insects and rodents. They should also be shelved several inches up from the floor and away from the wall. The pantry items, even paper goods, should be checked from time to time.

The job of everyone in the food industry is to avoid contamination of food during storage, preparation, and service. You need to develop a prescriptive approach to food handling using personal hygiene and kitchen cleanliness as a basis.

People are a big cause of cross-contamination. It often embarrasses people to discuss the importance of hand-washing after toilet use. It is, sad to say, one of the biggest sources of food contamination. Basic hygiene will prevent carrying microorganisms from the bathroom to the food. Hands should also be washed continuously while preparing food to avoid pollution from raw food to cooked. If you are wearing gloves, either change them, or wash your gloved hands frequently. Disposable gloves are to be used for all food that is not to be cooked.

One of your best investments will be several food thermometers. Temperature control is the most successful way to manage food borne illness. The rule of thumb is that any food needing refrigeration should never be at room temperature for more than an hour, a maximum of two, before serving.

Make it a principle to keep frozen food at below 0°F; cold food cold, under 40°F; and hot food, hot at 165°F. The refrigerator temperature must keep food between 32°F and 40°F. Poultry, fish, and meat, including cold cuts and smoked meat, should be kept under 37°F; milk, butter, cheese, and eggs, not over 40°F. (Before serving, butter can be held for several hours at 50°F.) Most fruit, salad, vegetables, and desserts can do well up to 45°F. Cover and label everything—you don't want to contaminate cooked food with raw. Freezer temperature has to be between 0°F to −15°F for frozen poultry, meat, and fish, frozen fruits and vegetables, and ice cream and other frozen desserts. Make sure you have one thermometer in the refrigerator and one to test with. Avoid the danger zone of 40°F to 140°F.

When storing food, use shallow storage containers to present a large surface area, and place in freezer or refrigerator as soon as possible. The idea of cooling hot foods first is a dangerous idea left over from the era of iceboxes, when hot food would melt the ice, lowering the cooling efficiency of the icebox. Large quantity food tasks have to be performed with an awareness of food safety. The danger zone is 40°F to 140°F. Defrost frozen food in the refrigerator, the microwave (following manufacturer's instructions), under running cold water, or cold water that is changed every thirty minutes. Cook within two hours.

For hot foods, the minimum guideline to hold them safely is an internal temperature of 165°F until they are served. Of course most have to be cooked at higher temperatures. By and large, cooking temperatures always mean internal temperatures from 160°F to

180°F for poultry, but they must be regulated on an item-by-item basis. During boiling, baking, and roasting, bacteria and parasites, including the ubiquitous salmonella, are killed. A probe thermometer is your best tool. Usually food is served well under the hour or two holding time. Maintaining the temperature for occasions like buffet service is to make sure the water in steam-table dishes is 180°F, and food placed in it is at 165°F. If neither method is available, refrigerate or freeze immediately for future service. Mishandled food has to be discarded, so it is important to make sure all the people you work with understand the rules. Remember there are many thousands of foodservice establishments run all over the world doing a remarkable job of providing safe meals with just a handful of regulations, but those are strictly adhered to.

Microwaves have become a part of the culinary scene. Safe installation, an attached probe, and a turntable are basic considerations for food safety. Glass, designated ceramic, and Pyroceram cooking utensils are preferred. Plastic should not touch food as the interaction of unapproved chemicals have not been fully analyzed yet. Avoid the use of leftover cold storage containers in the microwave. Plastic wrap, which is often recommended to cover food containers in the microwave, should never touch the food. Follow the manufacturer's instructions and avail yourself of most of their 800 hotline numbers as well. There is still some trial and error in microwave cooking but it can be a useful tool. Use both the attached internal meat probe thermometer for large amounts of food and your own meat thermometer if in doubt. Debone large pieces of meat or poultry, cover to hold in moisture, try to use mid-range levels for longer times to insure thorough cooking, turn several times, stir several times. It is often recommended that food stand to complete cooking time. Never partially cook and wait to finish. Never attempt to roast stuffed whole chicken or turkey in the microwave. Hot food hot, cold food cold, everything clean, that's it.

When I spoke to an official at the New York State Department of Health, Sanitation, and Food Protection, he said he had a terrific anecdote for this book. A private caterer in upstate New York had a party for sixty, and forty became ill. I thought that was no way to introduce a subject and that it was simply a scare tactic. The truth is, it highlights the fact that this is a very rare event because with care, it is virtually avoidable. Healthy people are pretty sturdy and do not need food that is surgically sterile, just kitchen clean. If you are preparing food for the very young or the very old, special attention must be paid. It cannot go without saying that if any guest is ill, or in a weakened condition, they might require a special meal.

Food Sanitation Procedures

Safe food means attention must be paid 100 percent of the time to twelve things:

1. Wash hands for at least thirty seconds with soap after using the bathroom.
2. Food handlers should not work when they have a contagious illness, even a cold, and any cuts or lesions should be well covered.
3. Keep work spaces clean.
4. Never let cooked food come in contact with raw poultry, meat, fish, eggs, or their juices.
5. Wash for thirty seconds any surface on which raw poultry, meat, fish, eggs, or their juices have been, including hands and knives.
6. Keep frozen food under 0°F.
7. Defrost frozen food in the refrigerator or microwave, and cook or serve within one hour.
8. Keep cold food under 40°F.
9. Keep hot food at an internal temperature of 165°F.
10. Transport and store hot foods hot and cold foods cold.
11. Serve food within one hour of removal from heat or cold.
12. Keep food storage and service areas free of insects and rodents.

FOOD SAFETY AND HANDLING

American Council on Science and Health
"Food Safety" booklet available—under $5.00
1995 Broadway
New York, NY 10023
Phone: (212) 362-7044

American Frozen Food Institute
Maclean, VA
Phone: (703) 821-0771

Health Academy
Field Services of the New York Health Department
160 West 100 Street
New York, NY 10025
Phone: (212) 280-9209

Hostline
School of Hotel Administration
Cornell University
G80 Statler Hall
Ithaca, NY 14853-6901
Phone: (607) 255-9992
Administrative and management hospitality database

Human Nutrition Information Service
6505 Belcrest Road
Room 325-A
Hyattsville, MD 20782
Phone: (301) 436-8617

Local Contacts
(In telephone directory)
State Department of Education
State Department of Health, Field Services

National Restaurant Association
Information and Library
1200 17 Street, N.W.
Washington, DC 20036
Phone: (800) 424-5156

New York Department of Health
  Publications
  Box 2000
  Albany, NY 12220

United States Department of Agriculture
  Food Safety and Inspection Service
  Washington, DC 20005
  (Catering-specific newsletters)
  Phone: (202) 690-0351

United States Department of Agriculture
  Food and Nutrition Information Center
  10301 Baltimore Boulevard
  Beltsville, MD 20705
  Phone: (301) 504-5719 / Fax: (301) 504-5472
  (Sanitary Codes and Food Nutrition and Protection Manuals)

United States Department of Agriculture
  Room 1163 South
  Washington, DC 20250
  Phone: (800) 535-4555; (202) 720-3333
  (Meat and Poultry Hotline information)
  Both numbers are accessible by Telecommunications for the
    Deaf

United Fresh Fruit and Vegetable Association
  727 North Washington Street
  Alexandria, VA 22314
  Phone: (800) 336-7745; (703) 836-3410 /
    Fax: (703) 836-7745

United States Government Printing Office
  710 North Capitol Street, N.W.
  Washington, DC 20401
  Phone: (202) 512-0132 / Fax: (202) 512-1355

University of Wisconsin
Dr. Dean O. Cliver
Food Research Institute
1925 Willow Drive
Madison, WI 53706
Phone: (608) 263-6937 / Fax: (608) 263-1114

TEN

Menus

O ne of the things that makes catering different from restaurant service is that the visual appearance of the meal must be created on the spot. A customer can look at a restaurant and see if it is the right place for their party, but when you cater you must assure your client that everything will be not only delicious but presented in an organized and attractive way. Though they haven't the time or perhaps the skills to prepare and present food themselves, the public is informed about food through travel, television, and magazines. There is enthusiasm about American and regional specialties from fast food to four-star, and the cuisines of various countries have become mainstream. The menu is the way to show them you know what they like.

People turn to a professional because it is difficult for them to visualize a meal down to the smallest detail and they want maximum results with a minimum of worry. The individuals or groups who come to you for catering services are eager to read your menus and talk about food. No one is shy or indifferent about the subject, particularly when they are inviting guests. It is not enough that you know you can deliver, you must convince the public. Catering means TLC.

Even if you and your cooking are known, your visual presentation is the selling tool that will attract them and hold their imagination. The menu is the page on which you create the events, from dream meals to calorie counters, that you are being paid for. It should excite, enthuse, and inspire confidence. It is necessary to have an array of menus prepared before you meet with the client. They are your portfolio and the key to successful merchandising.

From your point of view the key to accomplishment is proper cost analysis. You need to know how much it will cost to deliver the various menus and be prepared to offer substitutes that are appropriate for the budget. Be ready to present an item in a new way or to eliminate it entirely. You must have a breakdown of all the food items listed separately, for your eyes only, that tells you at a glance the comparative price of five pounds chicken or veal, rice, or potatoes. Remember you are in business to make a profit and still be competitive. A fully analyzed menu puts complete cost control at your fingertips. As soon as you know the number of people you are expected to serve, you need only a calculator to work from your price list.

Listen to your customer and make notes. If there is a lavish budget, each menu may be enhanced. Caviar, oysters, and champagne can always be added, as well as hothouse fruits and vegetables out of season. Time-consuming, individually made hors d'oeuvres, miniature desserts, and other labor-intensive dishes can be included, too.

More often, unfortunately, you will spend time trimming costs. A freshly tossed salad of inexpensive greens with the very best oil and vinegar is more memorable than endive poorly prepared. Make a large rectangular cake or tart and cut it into twenty-five portions rather than bake individual ones. Eliminate the appetizer and/or the soup. It is important to maintain a positive attitude about these alternatives and additions so that your client is assured they will have a beautifully presented spread. Steaming mugs of delicious soup, fresh salad, and savory sandwiches can be more fun than skimpy portions of expensive ingredients.

Keep updated with the availability of fresh foods in your area; fish, fruit, and vegetables vary with the seasons. It is vital to your reputation that you don't promise what you can't deliver. Pay attention to price updates. Large food companies list prices weekly, but most do it once a month. Dairy prices fluctuate regularly as do specialty items. Always ask the purveyor or distributor the price of each item when you place your order. Never assume it is the same as it was the last time you looked. No financial detail is too small to deserve your attention.

Remember, when you calculate costs you have to add rental items, special services, and nonfood items.

Menus change more than recipes do. Fashions and trends are reflected in menus, but the largest number of items on them are still tried and true favorites with some new accessories. This makes your job easier than it looks because you will have the recipes in your file. Read the food pages of your local papers each week to keep up with food in the news. Many of your patrons will get some of their ideas from those pages. Keep in mind that menu strategy is essential not only for breakfast, lunch, and dinner arrangements, but to organize everything from cocktail parties to children's birthdays, receptions, barbecues, weddings, and holiday celebrations. You will receive requests that range from down-home to casual elegance with a rare call for a traditionally formal affair.

The menu sets the mood. It also helps the client clarify exactly what they want and gives you an opportunity to make the notes that will serve as your outline for the specific job. It also opens the channels of communication in-house and establishes the basis for your staff, schedule, shopping list, nonfood needs, preparation, and cleanup. Keep each menu used and mark it with the client's name, the date, how many people were served, and the location. Make a brief memo of the cost and fee paid. Take snapshots or Polaroids. These will become part of your records so that your file will build and each successive job will be easier to estimate.

When you discuss menus with a customer be prepared for individual preferences. A simple way to discuss alternatives is course by course. Are hors d'oeuvres and appetizers both required? Soup? (Remember it is not only the price of the soup, but the extra prep time, setting pieces, and service.) Do you have to bake special bread, rolls, biscuits, and muffins, or will store-bought suffice? Regular bread? Crudités and salad? Will the entrée(s) have to be prepared as individual portions, or will they be carved from a whole roast or served from a chafing dish? Do guests get a choice of entrée? Will there be several relishes and accompaniments? Vegetables prepared simply or elaborately? Will there be fruit and cheese? Desserts have to be thought out carefully. Beverages must be planned in detail.

This is a good time to inquire about whether the service will be sit-down or buffet, or a combination. One possibility is hors d'oeuvres and appetizers as a buffet, or after a sit-down meal guests are offered coffee and dessert from a buffet.

Your own recipe files will be a quick reference for you to calculate food prices on your job cost chart. If you price each menu out for ten, twenty-five, and fifty people, you will be able to give your client a quick guesstimate. Some of the computer programs available for this are very helpful. Strawberries out of season are not in everybody's budget. Apple tarts with a shiny raspberry glaze are a delicious alternative. Remember though, that while ten individual tarts are not much more labor than two large ones, fifty individual ones will be more costly than fresh strawberries. Volume is as important as cost when figuring your fixed and variable expenses in order to arrive at your selling price. If you are ever on the spot, a rough rule of thumb is to offer a dish at four times the cost of the food itself.

If you envision each menu as a reflection of a recognizable special time that has easily identifiable foods and symbols, you will be able to provide your patrons with food and feeling they can rely on for their catered spreads. Go for the obvious unless begged not to. Thanksgiving without turkey, cranberry sauce, and some form of pumpkin is undistinguished. The quality of the preparation, special touches, and visual presentation are what make a meal memorable, not peculiarities.

Make sure the menus are clean and printed clearly. Computer printers do a professional job, but if yours is not set up yet, the local copy shop will reproduce them up on quality paper. If you have a special logo, use it. If not, have your name printed boldly across the top, and make sure your address and phone number are printed somewhere on it as well. You can make your menu distinctive by drawing a border on it or having blanks specially printed so that you can fill them in as you need them.

Use only four to six menus for any one meeting. Too many choices will only confuse your client. You must guide them and help them make a satisfactory decision. Early in the interview you will ascertain how knowledgeable they are, and how involved they want to be in the planning. It is your self-assurance and expert opinion that they are counting on and most of the final choices are yours. The following menus cover many occasions that caterers are called upon to provide for. These menus offer, for the most part, a fixed choice of main dishes. Use them as they are, or make them your own by adding or replacing your favorite dishes.

As a printing service for people who have various visual impairments, The Lighthouse Incorporated will duplicate any menu, invitation, or program in Braille or large-print text. The service generally takes a week to ten days and will increase the pleasure of any client or guest who would otherwise be unable to refer to printed material. The average price is $5.50 per page. Contact them at:

The Lighthouse Incorporated
800 Second Avenue
New York, NY 10017
Phone: (212) 808-0077

SAMPLE MENUS

New Year's Buffet

Easter Dinner

Passover Seder

Fourth of July Picnic

Thanksgiving Dinner

Christmas Eve Supper

Christmas Day Dinner

Wedding Reception

Graduation Party

Children's Birthday Party

Executive Luncheon

Library Fund-Raiser

Summer Garden Buffet

Summer Dinner

Autumn Lunch

Harvest Dinner

Winter Dinner

Spring Dinner

Chinese-Style Buffet

An Indian Curry Buffet

A French Dinner

An Italian Dinner

Santa Fe Supper

Southern Hospitality

California Calorie Counter

New Orleans-Style

An American Tradition

NEW YEAR'S BUFFET

Madeira Consommé

Crinkled Chèvre Cups
Assorted Small Muffins and Breads
Flavored Butters
Sweet and Savory Confitures
Stuffed Hard-Cooked Egg Whites
Smoked Salmon Triangles*
Shredded Vegetable Slaw Vinaigrette*
Mini Blinis with Caviar*

Winter Fruit Compote
Raspberry Floating Island
Angel Food Cake*

Coffee   Tea   Mineral Water
Fresh-Squeezed Orange Juice
Mimosas   Bellinis
Champagne   Champagne Cocktails

NOTES: (Recommendations for visual presentation and service of each course, including substitutes and alternatives. Suggestions for buffet stations, table settings, dishes, flatware, glassware, linens, and decorations.)

*Recipe given

EASTER DINNER

Assorted Smoked Fish

Easter Eggs in Bread Nests

Asparagus and Sweet Red and Yellow Pepper Salad

Beet-Tangerine Salad*

Roast Lamb with Rosemary and Juniper

Squash Blossoms in Batter

Sweet and Sour Lentils

Pashka

Pascal Cake

Vanilla Fruit Salad

Coffee   Tea

Mineral Water

Assorted Juices

Wine

NOTES:

*Recipe given

PASSOVER SEDER

Traditional Seder Plate

Gefilte Fish with Horseradish Dressing

Chicken Soup with Matzoh Balls

Brisket of Beef
Sautéed Spinach
Tzimmes

Lemon-Walnut Soufflé Cake
Assorted Sorbets, Almond Macaroons

Coffee   Tea
Mineral Water
Passover Wine

NOTES:

FOURTH OF JULY PICNIC

Summer Hors D'Oeuvres*

Iced Cucumber and Shrimp Soup

Chicken Salad*
Pasta Salad with Leeks Spinach and Mint*
Broccoli Salad with Egg Crespelle*
Tomato Salad with Fresh Basil
Assorted Breads, Breadsticks*

American-Flag Cake
Vanilla Mousse
Raspberry and Blueberry Sauce

Iced Coffee   Iced Tea
Mineral Water
Fruit Punch

NOTES:

*Receipe given

THANKSGIVING DINNER

Quick Caviar Spirals*
Endive and Radicchio Leaves
Hummus*
Dipping Sauce* in a Hollow Pumpkin
Miniature Muffins (Pumpkin*, Cranberry, Double-Corn,
Herb, Apple)
Flavored Butter and Fruit Butter

Roast Turkey with Mushroom-Giblet Gravy
Sausage, Chestnut, and Mushroom Stuffing
Cranberry-Beet Compote*
Tiny Onions and Raisins in Cassis
Baked Broccoli Puree
Maple Crisped Sweet Potatoes

Pecan Pie
Pumpkin-Mousse Pie

Coffee   Tea
Cider
Mineral Water
Fruit Wine

NOTES:

*Recipe given

CHRISTMAS EVE SUPPER

Savory Puffs and Fritters

Seafood Bisque

Assorted Small Breads*

Tangy Halibut, with Quick Tapenade*
Piquant Sweet Potatoes*
Scallops with Angel Hair Pasta in Lemon Cream Sauce*
Winter Green Salad with Sun-Dried Tomato-Hazelnut Dressing

Chestnut Trifle

Coffee   Tea
American Mineral Water
Wine

NOTES:

*Recipe given

CHRISTMAS DAY DINNER

Smoked Scallops and Shrimp
Red and Green Crudités
Roasted Eggplant Dip*

Saffron Buns

Naturally Cured Ham*
Maple Glazed Apples, Pears, and Onions*
Sautéed Brussels Sprouts and Chestnuts*
Roasted Root Vegetables*
Cranberry Sauce with Kumquats and Dried Cherries
Pumpkin-Ginger Mousse*

Basket of Miniature Fruits
Walnut Eggnog Cake*
Bûche de Noël

Coffee   Tea
Mineral Water
Eggnog   Wine   Assorted Liqueurs

NOTES:

*Recipe given

WEDDING RECEPTION

Assorted Hot and Cold Hors d'Oeuvres*

Miniature Rolls

Whole Poached Salmon* with Sauce Mousseline*
Cucumber-Dill Dressing*

Fresh Fruit Salad on Bed of Mesclun

Crisp Duck à l'Orange*
Wild Rice and Mushrooms*
Asparagus Drizzled with Cream*

Strawberries and Whipped Cream
Wedding Cake with Edible Gold Leaf and Flowers
Chocolate Champagne Truffles

Coffee   Tea
Open Bar
Mineral Water
Poured White and Red Wines
Champagne Toast

NOTES:

*Recipe given

GRADUATION PARTY

Roland Park Foolproof Pizza*
Caesar Salad*
Assorted Breads
Spaghetti with Rich Tomato-Mushroom Sauce*
Baked Ziti with Four Cheeses*

Fruit

Brownies, Chocolate-Chip Cookies
Popsicle™ Swirls

Mineral Water
Fresh Fruit Drinks
Iced Tea

NOTES:

* Recipe given

CHILDREN'S BIRTHDAY PARTY

Painted Cookie Place Cards

Carrot and Grapes Salad

Assorted Cut-Out Sandwiches
Salmon Burgers* with Cranberry Ketchup*
Miniature Vegetables

Carousel Birthday Cake
Individually Molded Ice Cream

Flavored Skim Milk
Fresh Fruit Punch
Mineral Water

NOTES:

* Recipe given

EXECUTIVE LUNCHEON

Wild-Mushroom Soup

Mixed Green Salad

Assorted Small Biscuits*

Salmon Steaks*
Onion Jam*
Saffron Noodles*
Steamed Broccoli and Cauliflower

Individual Fruit Tarts
Fresh-Fruit Basket

Coffee   Tea
Mineral Water
Wine

NOTES:

*Recipe given

LIBRARY FUND-RAISER

Emile Zola's Charcuterie (Le Ventre de Paris)

Tennyson's Dusky Loaves

Lewis Carroll's Soup of the Evening

Hemingway Lake Trout
John Hersey's Bluefish
Thomas Jefferson's Nouilly a Macaroni
Vegetables Alexandre Dumas
Veal Escalopes Colette
Mushroom Pudding Mrs. Joseph Conrad

Gertrude Stein's A Rose Is a Rose Sorbet and Lemon Ice Cream
Proust's Madeleines*

Coffee   Tea   Mineral Water
Champagne Cocktails
Wine

NOTES:

*Recipe given

SUMMER GARDEN BUFFET

Iced Fresh-Tomato Soup*

Deviled Eggs
Curried Charred Shrimp*
Assorted Biscuits*

Saffron Rice Seafood Salad*

Vegetables à la Grecque*
Skewered Chicken with Blueberry Dipping Sauce*
Roasted Potato Salad*
Corn and Barley Salad*

Berry Summer Pudding*
Melon Fruit Basket

Iced Coffee   Iced Tea
Mineral Water
Wine-Fruit Punch

NOTES:

*Recipe given

Summer Dinner

Mixed Local Summer Field Salad

Pasta Salad Niçoise*

Small Crusty French Rolls

Regional Bouillabaisse*

Steamed Corn

Coleslaw*

White-Bean Salad*

Assorted Sorbets with Fresh Fruit

Pastel Petits Fours*

Coffee   Tea

Mineral Water

Regional Wine

NOTES:

*Recipe given

Autumn Lunch

Chicken Liver Salad*

Pumpkin Soup*
Zucchini Bread

Balsamic Roasted Pork with Prunes*
Sautéed Apples and Fennel
Polenta

Persimmon Pudding
Chocolate and Chocolate Cake*

Coffee   Tea
Mineral Water
Wine

NOTES:

*Recipe given

HARVEST DINNER

Crab-Cake Bites with Maryland Crab Dipping Sauce*

Minestrone*

Assorted Grain Breads

Pan-Roasted Red Snapper*
Stuffed Small Squash
Andean Potatoes*

Bourbon-Pecan Bread Pudding*

Coffee   Tea
Mineral Water
Cider

NOTES:

*Recipe given

WINTER DINNER

Alaska Shrimp Salad*

Deep-Green Split-Pea Soup*

Bread Basket*

Chicken Breasts Stuffed with Chèvre and Sun-Dried Tomatoes*
Polenta Squares*
Tomato Coulis*
Zucchini in Lemon-Mint Butter*

Winter Fruits
Chocolate Terrine in White-Chocolate Blizzard*

Coffee   Tea
Water
Wine

NOTES:

*Recipe given

SPRING DINNER

Endive, Watercress, and Citrus Salad

Wild-Mushroom Soup

Assorted Small Breads

Tuna Medallions*
Cubed Potatoes*
Stir-Fried Broccoli*

Strawberry Shortcake

Coffee   Espresso   Tea
Mineral Water
Wine

NOTES:

*Recipe given

CHINESE-STYLE BUFFET

Assorted Steamed Dumplings
Skewered Pork and Papaya*
Plum Dipping Sauce*
Spiced Roasted Nuts*

Sweet and Sour Fish*
Szechuan Chicken Breasts*
Eggplants and Apricots*
Stir-fried Snow Peas, Carrots, and Water Chestnuts*
Cold Sesame Noodles*
Rice with Black Mushrooms

Assorted Small Cakes
Citrus Salad

Mineral Water
Wine and Beer

NOTES:

*Recipe given

AN INDIAN CURRY BUFFET

Assorted Indian Breads (Paratha, Chapati, Puri)

Samosas (Filled Savory Pastries)
Pakoras (Vegetable Fritters)
Dosai (Stuffed Pancakes)
Peas and Panir
Lentil Salad*
Beef Curry*
Shrimp and Cashew Curry
Peach Chutney*
Saffron Rice*
Seasoned Yogurt

Wild-Rice Carrot Cake*

Coffee   Tea
Mineral Water
Wine
Beer

NOTES:

*Recipe given

A FRENCH DINNER

Hot Hors d'Oeuvres*
Duck Rillettes*

Crostini*
French Bread, Butter

Consommé à la Reine

Filet Mignon Roast with Madeira Sauce*
Braised Endive
Pommes Anna
Leaf-Lettuce Salad

Individual Vacherins (Fruit Mousse in Meringue)
Coupe aux Marrons
Curled Almond Tiles*

Coffee   Tea
Mineral Water
Wine

NOTES:

*Recipe given

AN ITALIAN DINNER

Antipasti Misti
Caponata*

Fennel with Shaved Parmesan*

Italian Bread, Bruschetta* Breadsticks*

Chicken Scalloppa with Porcini Mushrooms
Spinach with Shallots, Pine Nuts, and Raisins*
Saffron Risotto*
Arugula Salad with Lemon-Walnut Dressing

Assorted Italian Cheeses

Semifreddo
Mixed Berries
Almond Biscotti*

Espresso Cappuccino
Italian Mineral Water
Italian Wine Tasting

NOTES:

*Recipe given

SANTA FE SUPPER

Guacamole,*—Salsa, Tortilla Chips
Corn-Bread Sticks,* Jalapeño Jam
Blue-Corn Muffins, Herbed Honey

Turkey Chili Mole*
Taco Salad*
Posole, New Mexican Style*
Fried Plantain Chips*

Chocolate and Chocolate Cake*
Piñon Ice Cream

Iced Chocolate, Cappuccino, and Herb Teas
Mineral Water
Pitchers of Beer and Sangrita†
†(mixture of tomato juice, grenadine, orange juice, lime, and
tequila)

NOTES:

*Recipe given

SOUTHERN HOSPITALITY

Tossed Salad with Edible Flowers

She-Crab Soup

Assorted Benne Rolls, Flavored Butters and Spreads

Southern-Fried Chicken in Biscuit Batter
Baked Yams
Sautéed Greens

Key Lime Sorbet
Peach Ice Cream
Pecan Pie

Coffee   Tea
Mineral Water
Virginia Wines

CALIFORNIA CALORIE COUNTER

Tangerine and Watercress Salad

Mushroom Consommé
Assorted Toasts

Baked Salmon Fillets on Roasted Tomatoes*
Steamed Baby Vegetables

Walnut Meringue Kisses
Raspberry Soufflé

Espresso   Tea
Mineral Water
Wine Spritzers

NOTES:

*Recipe given

NEW ORLEANS-STYLE

Crawfish Gratin

Sweet-Potato Bread

Blackened Catfish
Gumbo*
Plain White Rice*
Pickled Vegetable Salad
Hush Puppies

Savory Sorbets
Mocha Cream Cake
Miniature Pralines

Coffee   Tea
Mineral Water
Wine

NOTES:

*Recipe given

AN AMERICAN TRADITION

Mixed Green Salad

Assorted Biscuits and Muffins, Flavored Butters and Spreads

Clam Chowder*

Whole Maple-Roasted Chickens
Corn Bread-Pecan Stuffing
Classic Boston Baked Beans*
Minted Carrots and Peas

Apple/Cherry Pies
Vanilla Ice Cream

Coffee   Tea
American Mineral Water
Regional American Wines

NOTES:

*Recipe given

Recipe File

Hors D'Oeuvres and Appetizers

MINI BLINIS WITH CAVIAR

- 1 envelope active dry yeast
- 1 teaspoon sugar
- ½ cup warm water
- 1 cup unbleached all-purpose flour
- 2 cups buckwheat flour
- 1 cup buttermilk
- 1 cup water
- 2 eggs, separated
- 1 teaspoon baking soda
- ½ cup molasses
- 5 tablespoons sweet butter, melted and cooled butter for skillet
- 1 pint sour cream (optional)
- 8 ounces caviar or small red salmon roe

Proof yeast with sugar in warm water for 10 minutes.

Incorporate mixed flours, buttermilk, and water to yeast mixture. Cover and let stand for 1 hour or refrigerate for 4 to 8 hours until ready to cook.

Beat egg whites until stiff and set aside. Add baking soda to molasses and set aside. Beat egg yolk and melted butter into batter and then incorporate molasses and egg whites. Drop by tablespoonfuls onto lightly buttered griddle or skillet. Cook till edges bubble. Turn blini and cook about 30 seconds longer. Remove to warm platter and top each with ½ teaspoon caviar.

If desired, first place teaspoon of sour cream on blini. Plain blinis may be kept in warm oven but are best served immediately.

Yield: 40.

JALAPEÑO-CHEESE WAFERS

5 ounces Monterey jack cheese with jalapeño peppers, grated (1¼ cups)
¾ cup all-purpose flour
5 tablespoons sweet butter, at room temperature

Combine cheese, flour, and butter. Shape into a 1½-inch-thick log approximately 8 inches long. Roll in plastic wrap and refrigerate 1 hour or until firm.

Preheat oven to 350°F. Line baking sheets with aluminum foil. Slice dough to ⅛-inch thickness. Place on prepared baking sheets.

Bake for 12 minutes or until edges are slightly browned. Remove with spatula and cool slightly before serving. It may be necessary to peel foil away.

Yield: 50.

SMOKED SALMON TRIANGLES

25 slices packaged thin-sliced pumpernickel or rye bread
12 ounces cream cheese
 3 tablespoons sour cream
 2 tablespoons red horseradish
 2 lemons
 8 ounces smoked salmon
50 capers, drained
   olives
   parsley, and lemon slices for garnish

Trim crusts from bread and cut in half diagonally. Mix cream cheese, sour cream, and undrained horseradish. Spread thinly on bread.

Trim ends from lemons and slice paper-thin with a food processor or a very sharp knife. Cut slices into wedges. Cut salmon slices into triangles and place on cheese mixture. Top each with a piece of lemon and a caper.

Accompany with assorted olives and garnish with parsley and lemon slices.

Yield: 50.

CRINKLED CHÈVRE CUPS

 1 pound fresh or frozen phyllo dough, thawed
 3 ounces sun-dried tomatoes
 2 chèvre logs (9 ounces each)
 1 cup (2 sticks) unsalted butter, melted

Preheat oven to 350°F. Butter a baking sheet.

Unroll thawed phyllo on flat surface, and cover with waxed paper, then a damp clean kitchen towel, to prevent them from drying out.

Mince sun-dried tomatoes and pour 1 cup hot water over. Cut each chèvre log in quarters lengthwise, and each quarter into 6 pieces. Drain tomatoes and place on flat dish.

Place a sheet of phyllo on flat work surface and brush with melted butter. Fold in half and butter surface. Press some tomato pieces around cheese. Center cheese on folded phyllo and wrap dough once tightly then again loosely around cheese so that outside resembles crumpled paper. Brush lightly with butter and place on prepared baking sheet. Repeat with remaining ingredients.

Bake for 15 minutes or until golden brown.

Carefully cut in half and serve cheese-side up. They may be frozen before baking and baked just before serving.

Yield: 48.

CRAB-CAKE BITES

  2 celery stalks
  2 whole eggs
¼ cup mayonnaise
¼ cup dry white wine
  1 teaspoon freshly ground black pepper
½ teaspoon coarse (kosher) salt
¼ teaspoon cayenne pepper
1½ pounds cooked crabmeat, flaked
  2 cups unsalted cracker crumbs
  1 large onion, grated
¼ cup minced fresh parsley
    whites from 2 eggs
  3 tablespoons olive oil
  3 tablespoons unsalted butter
    Maryland Crab Dipping Sauce (recipe, page 150)

Remove strings from celery and cut into small dice. In large bowl, mix whole eggs, mayonnaise, wine, black pepper, salt, and cayenne pepper. Add crabmeat, cracker crumbs, onion, celery, and parsley. Whisk egg whites until foamy, then fold into crab mixture.

Heat oil and butter in large skillet and drop tablespoonfuls of crab cakes into hot pan. Cook 3 minutes or until browned. Turn and cook 2 or 3 minutes on the other side. Drain on paper towels. (These may be made in an electric fryer according to manufacturer's directions.)

Serve with Maryland Crab Dipping Sauce.

Yield: 50.

MARYLAND CRAB DIPPING SAUCE

   1 cup mayonnaise
  ½ cup prepared mild mustard
  ¾ cup ketchup
  ½ cup drained pickle relish
  ¼ cup bottled horseradish
   1 tablespoon Maryland crab seasoning
  ¼ to ½ teaspoon hot-pepper sauce

Mix ingredients and chill until ready to serve.

Yield: 3 cups.

DUCK RILLETTES

One 5-pound duck and duck liver
1 tablespoon coarse (kosher) salt
¼ teaspoon *each*
  ground cloves, nutmeg,
  cinnamon, coriander,
  white pepper,
  crumbled dried basil, and dried thyme
1 cup dry red wine
¼ cup cognac
6 shallots
  cornichons and warm Crostini (recipe, page 152)

Rub duck inside and out with salt and spice mixture, cover, and refrigerate overnight.

Preheat oven to 400°F. Quarter duck and place on rack over roasting pan. Roast 30 minutes. Drain fat and reserve in small saucepan. Continue roasting for 1½ hours. Remove duck to platter.

Turn heat off and add wine, cognac, and shallots to liquid and fat in roasting pan and stir. Return to oven until ready to use.

Remove skin from duck and mince. Debone meat and shred. Stir meat and skin into warm liquid in roasting pan. Transfer mixture to a ceramic bowl or 2-quart soufflé dish.

Refrigerate, covered, for 3 hours, stirring every 30 minutes. If after 3 hours there is not enough fat on the surface to coat the duck, cover with reserved fat in saucepan.

Cover and keep refrigerated. Just before serving, scrape surface fat away. Serve with cornichons and warm Crostini.

Yield: 2½ pounds.

CROSTINI

    6 12-ounce baguettes
    1 tablespoon mixed herbs like herbes de Provence
    ½ teaspoon coarse (kosher) salt
    ¾ cup olive oil

Preheat oven to 350°F. Slice bread into ¼-inch-thick slices. (If the baguettes are very narrow, cut on an angle.)

Mix herbs and salt. Arrange slices in a single layer on ungreased baking sheets. Drizzle with olive oil and sprinkle with herb blend.

Bake 10 minutes or until edges are golden brown. Serve warm with Duck Rillettes, if you wish.

Yield: 100.

SKEWERED CHICKEN WITH BLUEBERRY DIPPING SAUCE

    4 boneless, skinless chicken breasts (3 pounds)

    Marinade:
    1 tablespoon sesame oil
    1 tablespoon olive oil
    1 tablespoon curry powder
    1 teaspoon ground cumin
       pinch cayenne (optional)
    2 garlic cloves, minced
 1½ cups orange juice
    ½ cup low-sodium soy sauce
       Blueberry Dipping Sauce (recipe, page 153)

Slice chicken into thin strips and set aside.

For marinade, heat oils in saucepan over medium-low heat and stir in curry powder, cumin, and cayenne, stirring to keep from clumping or burning. Add garlic, but do not brown. Stir in orange juice and soy sauce and remove from heat.

Place chicken and marinade in shallow pan, cover, and refrigerate for 2 hours. Thread on wooden skewers that have been soaked in water.

Broil or grill 3 minutes on each side.

Serve warm with Blueberry Dipping Sauce.

Yield: 50.

BLUEBERRY DIPPING SAUCE

3 cups blueberries
1 whole lemon, seeded and minced
1 cup packed brown sugar
½ cup granulated sugar
⅔ cup raspberry or other berry vinegar
1 teaspoon ground allspice
1 teaspoon ground ginger

Combine ingredients in nonreactive saucepan and bring to boil. Lower heat and simmer 30 minutes, stirring frequently. Chill and serve as a dipping sauce or an accompaniment.

Yield: 1 pint.

CURRIED CHARRED SHRIMP

2 pounds shrimp, peeled and tails left on
¼ cup olive oil
¼ cup (½ stick) unsalted butter
3 tablespoons curry powder
1 teaspoon ground allspice
1 teaspoon paprika
candied kumquats for garnish

Mix oil, butter, and curry powder in a skillet over low heat. Stir in shrimp and cook for 3 minutes. Place under broiler 1 or 2 minutes until shrimp are slightly charred.

Drain on paper towels. Arrange on platter, and garnish with candied kumquats, if you wish.

Yield: 50.

SKEWERED PORK AND PAPAYA

2½   pounds boneless pork, cut in ¾-inch cubes
  3   cups low-sodium soy sauce
  1   cup honey
  ½   cup sherry
  ¼   cup minced peeled gingerroot
  2   large papayas, cut in ¾-inch cubes

Mix all ingredients except papaya. Marinate, covered, in the refrigerator for 3 hours. Add papaya and thread on skewers that have been soaked in water.

Broil or grill 8 minutes, turning occasionally.

Yield: 50.

PLUM DIPPING SAUCE

  8   ounces purple plums, pitted and minced
  1   cup ginger marmalade
  1   cup low-sodium soy sauce
  ¼   cup Chinese-style mustard

Combine all ingredients in nonreactive saucepan over low heat. Bring to slow boil, stirring occasionally. Remove from heat and serve warm or cold.

Yield: 1 pint.

GUACAMOLE

  6 large ripe avocados
  4 large ripe tomatoes
  6 garlic cloves, peeled
  2 tablespoons chili powder
  2 limes
  ½ cup minced cilantro leaves

Remove avocado skin and pits. Reserve pits.

Remove skins and seeds from tomatoes. (Skins can be removed by dipping tomatoes from fork into boiling water for 12 seconds. Pierce skin with paring knife and skin will pull back easily.)

In nonreactive bowl, dice tomatoes and fork-mash avocados until creamy and a little lumpy. Press garlic through a press and scrape liquid into mixture. Stir in chili powder. Squeeze juice from both limes and grate the zest of one into mixture stirring well. Top with minced cilantro.

If not serving immediately, insert avocado pits into guacamole, cover surface with plastic wrap, and refrigerate. Serve at room temperature with crisp baked corn- or wheat-tortilla chips.

Yield: 1 quart.

SPICED ROASTED NUTS

  3 cups whole almonds
  ½ cup packed brown sugar
  2 tablespoons safflower oil
  1 tablespoon crushed red pepper flakes

Preheat oven to 300°F. Mix all ingredients on nonstick baking sheet.

Bake for 10 minutes. Drain on paper towels. Serve warm.

Yield: 3 cups.

HOT HONEY PECANS

   3 tablespoons unsalted butter
   2 tablespoons honey
   ½ teaspoon hot-pepper sauce
   3 cups pecan halves

Melt butter in skillet over low heat. Add honey and pepper sauce. Stir in pecans until evenly coated. Remove from heat and let cool. Serve warmed in oven.

Yield: 3 cups.

CURRIED WALNUTS

   2 tablespoons unsalted butter
   2 tablespoons safflower oil
   2 teaspoons curry powder
   3 cups walnut halves

Preheat oven to 350°F. Heat butter and oil in small saucepan over low heat. Blend in curry powder, then add walnuts, stirring until well coated. Spread on baking sheet.

Bake for 10 minutes. Drain on paper towels.

Yield: 3 cups.

BLUE-CHEESE PUFFS

Pâte à Choux:

1 cup water
6 tablespoons unsalted butter
¼ teaspoon salt
1 cup "instant" flour
5 eggs

Blue-Cheese Filling:

8 ounces blue cheese, crumbled
3 ounces cream cheese, at room temperature
½ cup milk or nonfat plain yogurt
½ cup chopped walnuts
   confectioners' sugar

Preheat oven to 400°F. Butter foil-lined baking sheets and set aside.

In large saucepan over medium heat, bring water, butter, and salt to a boil. Remove from heat and add the flour, stirring until it forms a ball. Cool. Beat in eggs 1 at a time. Fill pastry bag and drop ½-inch pieces 2 inches apart on prepared baking sheets.

Bake 10 minutes. Lower oven temperature to 350°F and bake for 15 minutes longer.

Remove sheets from oven and *turn heat off*. Pierce puffs, then split them across. Replace top and return to oven for 15 minutes. Puffs may be frozen before or after filling and warmed in oven or microwave before serving.

For filling, blend cheeses with milk or yogurt smoothly and add chopped walnuts. Fill each puff and set on baking sheet. Warm in medium oven before serving. Place on platter and sprinkle with confectioners' sugar.

Yield: 50.

QUICK CAVIAR SPIRALS

3 frozen 9-inch pie shells, thawed
8 ounces cream cheese, at room temperature
¼ cup sour cream or milk
5 shallots, minced
6 ounces inexpensive black caviar

Preheat oven to 325°F. Butter two baking sheets.

Gently press pie shells flat. Mix cream cheese, sour cream, and shallots until smooth. Add sour cream or milk so that mixture spreads easily. Divide among three shells and spread evenly. Spread caviar in 5-inch band across each shell.

Starting with uncovered end, roll each shell jelly-roll fashion. Trim ends and cut in ½-inch slices. Set flat-side down on prepared baking sheets.

Bake for 20 minutes. Serve warm, not hot.

Yield: 50.

BRUSCHETTA

2 pounds Italian bread
7 large red peppers
1½ pounds mozzarella cheese, shredded (6 cups)
1½ cups finely chopped fresh basil leaves
1 cup olive oil
coarse (kosher) salt

Preheat oven to broil. Cut bread into ½-inch-thick slices. Arrange on baking sheets. Set aside.

Roast peppers under broiler until skins blacken and bubble. Place in paper bag, twist shut, and steam for 3 minutes. Peel and slice into thin strips.

Lower oven temperature to 350°F. Arrange cheese,

peppers, and basil on bread slices. Toast 5 minutes or until edges are golden brown. (May be topped with chopped, peeled, and seeded fresh tomatoes instead of peppers.) Drizzle with olive oil and coarse salt before serving.

Yield: 40.

CAPONATA

  2 medium onions
¾ cup (approximately) olive oil
  1 can (1 pound 13 ounces) tomato puree, or fresh equivalent
½ cup dry red wine
½ cup sugar
  2 eggplants, each about 9-inch long
¾ cup balsamic vinegar
  1 head celery
½ pound large pitted green olives
1½ ounces salted capers, rinsed
½ cup coarsely chopped Italian (flat-leaf) parsley

Cut onions into quarters, then slice. In a heavy 2-quart saucepan, cook onion in olive oil until transparent. Stir in tomato puree, wine, and sugar. Cook over medium heat until bubbly. Lower heat and simmer for 30 minutes or until sauce becomes dark and thick.

Wash eggplants and cut into large dice. Salt and place in colander set over large bowl or sink until moisture is extracted. Squeeze moisture out of the eggplant, using your hands or a square of cheesecloth. Heat olive oil in skillet large enough to hold eggplant in no more than two layers. Sauté 20 minutes or until tender. Add olive oil if needed.

Stir vinegar into tomato sauce, then add eggplant.

Cut celery 5 inches from root end and reserve tops for another use. Separate into stalks and remove strings. Cut into large dice and blanch. Drain and run under cold water to keep crisp. Pit and coarsely chop olives. Add capers, parsley, olives, and celery to tomato sauce and stir over low heat for 5 minutes.

Remove from heat and cool. Place in covered container and refrigerate. It will keep well for several days.

Yield: 20 servings.

HUMMUS

   3 cups cooked chick-peas
   1 cup tahina
   1 cup water
  ½ cup olive oil
    juice of 2 lemons
   3 tablespoons minced fresh parsley leaves
   3 tablespoons minced fresh mint leaves
    sprigs of parsley and mint for garnish

Mash chick-peas with a potato masher and set aside. Blend remaining ingredients until creamy. Add mashed chick-peas and blend. Harissa—a Middle Eastern pepper sauce—is often served with this. It is very hot.

Garnish with sprigs of parsley and mint and serve with crudités, pita or crackers.

Yield: 3 pints.

ROASTED EGGPLANT DIP

      4 large eggplants
      4 green bell peppers
      8 garlic cloves, peeled
    ½ cup olive oil
      1 teaspoon coarse (kosher) salt
    ¼ teaspoon black pepper
        pomegranate seeds for garnish
        toasted pita-bread triangles

Cook eggplants over direct flame or under broiler 20 minutes or until eggplants are runny, turning often to char skin. (As an alternative, cut eggplant in half lengthwise. Rub all over with olive oil and place cut-side down on sheet pan.)

Bake in 350°F oven for 45 minutes.

Cut eggplants in half and scrape flesh from skin into a large bowl. Discard skin.

Char green peppers, turning until skin is blackened. Place in paper bag twisted shut for several minutes until skin is steamed loose. Remove and discard skins and place flesh in bowl.

Chop eggplant and green peppers until minced and mushy. Squeeze garlic cloves through press (discard fibers that do not go through) into olive oil and mix with salt and pepper. Stir into eggplant and peppers. Cover and chill in refrigerator until ready to serve.

Garnish with pomegranate seeds just before serving. Serve with toasted pita-bread triangles.

Yield: 3 pints.

VEGETABLES À LA GRECQUE

1 cup water
2 cups dry white wine
1 cup olive oil
  juice of 2 lemons
  shells of 2 lemons
1 tablespoon dried thyme
6 bay leaves
4 sprigs fresh tarragon
4 garlic cloves stuck with several whole cloves
3 pounds mushrooms (small white)
3 pounds baby string beans, tipped
3 pounds mixed baby green and yellow zucchini
1 head cauliflower
2 pounds small white onions

Combine liquids, lemon shells, herbs, and garlic in
nonreactive saucepan. Add mushrooms, bring to a boil,
then simmer for 15 minutes. Remove with slotted spoon.

Add green beans, simmer 8 minutes, and remove.
Wash and dry zucchini and simmer for 6 minutes.
Separate cauliflower into florets. Peel onions and add
with florets to poaching sauce. Cook 20 minutes.

Arrange in rimmed platter, cover, and chill at least 2
hours before serving. Trim into bite-size pieces and
arrange on a bed of greens drizzled with drained sauce. It
is better to simmer vegetables separately, but if there is
no time, they can be put in the pot together.

Yield: 50 servings.

Salads

FENNEL WITH SHAVED PARMESAN

   6 large fennel bulbs
   ½ cup olive oil
   ½ teaspoon coarse (kosher) salt, (optional)
     freshly ground pepper and nutmeg
  10 ounces Parmesan cheese, shaved

Trim off narrow part of fennel and store in freezer for
another use. Cut bulb of fennel into quarters and slice
thinly with processor or by hand. Arrange fennel on
platter. Drizzle with olive oil and coarse salt. Top with
shaved Parmesan. Grind pepper and nutmeg over all
before serving.

Yield: 20 servings.

ALASKA SHRIMP SALAD

  12 heads endive
   1 cup mayonnaise
   1 cup nonfat plain yogurt
   1 cup marinated artichoke hearts, drained
   ⅓ cup pickle relish, drained
  1½ pounds cooked Alaska pink shrimp (about 400 tiny
     shrimp to pound)

Blend mayonnaise, yogurt, artichoke hearts, and relish.
Separate endive leaves and arrange on plates or platter.
Top each with artichoke sauce. Arrange shrimp over all.

Yield: 20 servings.

PASTA SALAD WITH LEEKS, SPINACH, AND MINT

> 3 pounds papardelle (1½-inch-square fresh pasta) or bow-tie pasta
> 5 leeks
> ⅔ cup olive oil
> 4 pounds fresh spinach, shredded
> ½ cup chopped mint leaves
>   salt and pepper to taste
>   freshly ground nutmeg

Boil pasta until tender, about 1 minute past al dente. Drain and place in bowl of cold water until ready to use.

Cut leeks lengthwise, cut off root, and slice into 1½-inch slices. Heat olive oil in large skillet and brown leeks. Turn off heat and stir in spinach and mint. Drain pasta and dry. Mix pasta and vegetables together with salt and pepper and chill. Grind nutmeg over pasta before serving.

Yield: 20 servings.

PASTA SALAD NIÇOISE

> 3 pounds multi-flavored spiral pasta
>   oil and vinegar
> 2 pounds fresh tuna
> 1 pound pitted ripe olives
> 1 pound diced boiled new potatoes
> ¼ cup drained capers
> 2 large red onions, diced
> 1 cup marinated or canned artichoke hearts, drained
> ½ cup marinated pimientos, diced & drained
>   lettuce leaves
>   hard-cooked eggs and anchovies for garnish

Boil and drain pasta following package directions. Run under cold water and dry. Toss with oil and vinegar and chill. Dice tuna and pan-broil until fish is firm and cooked. Mix pasta, tuna, olives, potatoes, capers, onions, artichokes, and pimientos in large salad bowl for buffet or plate individually over lettuce leaves, arranging ingredients in layers. Garnish with sliced eggs and anchovies.

Yield: 20 servings.

SAFFRON RICE SEAFOOD SALAD

    1 cup olive oil
    1 cup sherry vinegar
    1 cup minced shallots
    2 pounds cooked Alaska tiny shrimp
    2 pounds cooked small squid
    2 pounds cooked small scallops
    1 quart steamed mussels
    3 quarts cold saffron rice
    3 cups orange sections
      grated zest of 2 oranges
    1 large bunch Italian (flat-leaf) parsley, coarsely chopped
    2 pounds green peas, shelled

Mix together oil, vinegar, and shallots. Toss with the seafood. Mix saffron rice, orange sections, and zest. Top with seafood mixture. Mix parsley and peas. Place around salad.

Yield: 50 servings.

COLESLAW

  8 pounds cabbage
  2 pounds carrots, scraped
2⅔ cups raisins
  2 cups apple juice
  2 cups mayonnaise
  1 cup safflower oil
  1 cup vinegar
  2 tablespoons ground cumin
  3 tablespoons caraway seeds
     salt and pepper to taste

Shred cabbage and carrots. Plump raisins in apple juice. Drain and reserve juice for another use. Mix cabbage, carrots and raisins with remaining ingredients and stir.

Yield: 50 servings.

CHICKEN SALAD

  1 head celery
  2 pounds apples
  2 pounds pears
     iced water
     half a lemon
  3 yellow peppers, skinned and seeded
  3 bunches watercress
  9 pounds cooked boneless chicken breast
  2 cups walnut oil
  1 cup sherry vinegar
  2 ounces sprigs fresh tarragon
  4 garlic cloves, peeled and minced
10 shallots, minced
     freshly ground black pepper

1 pound walnut pieces
   small section of hot pepper to taste
   Italian (flat-leaf) parsley or cilantro for garnish

Separate celery stalks and carefully remove strings. Peel
and core apples and pears. Slice and reserve in iced water
with half a lemon in it. Slice celery and peppers. Cut
watercress into bite-size pieces. Drain fruit. Cube chicken.
Place preceding ingredients in large bowl.

Mix oil and vinegar with half the tarragon, garlic,
shallots, and pepper. Blend. Toss salad with oil and
vinegar mixture and stir in the rest of the fresh tarragon
and walnuts. Garnish with parsley or cilantro.

Yield: 50 servings.

ROASTED POTATO SALAD

12 pounds potatoes
 2 cups white wine vinegar
 3 cups olive oil
    several sprigs fresh rosemary
    salt and pepper to taste
 8 bunches scallions

Preheat oven to 375°F. Cut potatoes into 1-inch cubes
and coat with some of the olive oil. Place potatoes in
shallow baking pan. Place rosemary over. Roast for 20
minutes or until tender when pierced with a skewer.
Chop scallions and blend with remaining oil and the
vinegar. Toss scallion mixture with potatoes. Add salt and
pepper to taste.

Yield: 50 servings.

CHICKEN LIVER SALAD

     5 whole heads garlic
    ½ cup olive oil
     3 pounds chicken livers
     1 cup Marsala
       zest and juice of 2 oranges
    ¼ cup raspberry vinegar
     4 heads chicory
     8 ounces walnuts
    ½ cup minced parsley leaves

Rub garlic with some of the olive oil and place on baking sheet sprinkled with olive oil. Roast for 1 hour at 360°F. Clean chicken livers and remove all membranes. Sauté in oil and add Marsala. Lift livers from pan to be served warm.

Add orange juice and zest to oil and Marsala in pan. Stir and remove from heat. Add oil and vinegar and blend dressing in pan.

Rinse chicory and tear into bite-size pieces. On plates or platter, place bed of chicory, chicken livers, walnuts, and individual garlic cloves. Top with dressing. Garnish with parsley.

Yield: 20 servings.

COOKED CAESAR-SALAD DRESSING

     6 egg yolks
    ½ cup wine vinegar
       juice of 2 lemons
     1 teaspoon dry mustard
       dash Worcestershire sauce
     1 cup olive oil
    ½ cup safflower oil

Combine all ingredients except oils in a small heavy saucepan over low heat, whisking continuously. Raise heat to medium and keep stirring until mixture thickens and starts to bubble. Remove from heat and let cool. Stir occasionally. When cooled, whisk into oils until well blended. Dress salad or refrigerate until needed. Shake or whisk before using.

Yield: 3 cups.

CROUTONS

2 garlic cloves, peeled
3 tablespoons olive oil
4 slices white bread, crusts removed

Heat garlic in olive oil in skillet. Cut each slice of bread into 16 croutons and brown on all sides in oil. Remove and drain on paper towels. Depending on other courses, sprinkle over 1 to 2 cups greens per serving.

Yield: 5 dozen.

WHITE-BEAN SALAD

5 cups cooked white beans
1 cup toasted walnut pieces*
1 fennel bulb, diced
¼ cup walnut oil
½ cup olive oil
¼ cup sherry vinegar
4 yellow peppers, roasted
Italian flat-leaf parsley and lemon slices for garnish

*To toast walnuts: Preheat oven to 350°F. Spread nuts in a single layer on baking sheet. Bake for 15 minutes.

Mix all ingredients except roasted peppers. Cut peppers into strips and cover bean salad. Garnish with flat-leaf Italian parsley and lemon slices.

Yield: 20 servings.

TACO SALAD

  3 large heads lettuce
  2 bunches red radishes
  4 carrots, scraped
12 large ripe tomatoes
  4 large avocados
  2 pounds Monterey jack cheese
2½ pounds cooked chicken
  2 green chiles, seeded
  2 canned jalapeño peppers, or to taste
2½ cups prepared green salsa
20 corn tortillas, crisped
     sour cream for garnish

Shred lettuce, radishes, and carrots. Slice tomatoes and avocados. Julienne cheese and chicken. Finely dice chiles and jalapeños and mix with salsa.

On individual plates or all on platters, layer tortillas covered with lettuce, carrots, radishes, and tomatoes. Place chicken and cheese over salad. Top with avocados and pepper mixture. Garnish with dollops of sour cream.

Yield: 20 servings.

BEET-TANGERINE SALAD

4 pounds medium beets
4 pounds medium-small onions
¾ cup ginger marmalade

½ cup cider vinegar
¼ cup olive oil
1 tablespoon prepared mustard
　salt and pepper to taste
10 tangerines, peeled and sectioned

Preheat oven to 400°F. Scrub beets and trim off leaves to ½ inch of stem end. Do not peel onions. Bake beets and onions for 45 minutes to 1 hour until vegetables can be pierced with a knife. While beets and onions are still warm, peel them and slice.

In small saucepan heat marmalade, vinegar, oil, mustard, and salt and pepper, stir until blended. With warm mixture, dress beets, onions, and tangerine sections and chill.

Yield: 20 servings.

LENTIL SALAD

1½ pounds lentils
¼ cup olive oil
3 red onions, diced
2 cucumbers, peeled, seeded, and diced
　salt and pepper to taste
2 tablespoons dried fines herbes
10 ounces chèvre cheese, like Montrachet
1 bunch Italian (flat-leaf) parsley, chopped

Bring lentils to a boil and cook for 20 minutes or until tender. Cool and stir in oil, onions, cucumbers, salt and pepper to taste, and herbes. Top with crumbled chèvre and parsley.

Yield: 20 servings.

SHREDDED VEGETABLE SLAW VINAIGRETTE

    3 pounds broccoli
    6 carrots, scraped
    4 turnips
    1 small head red cabbage

       Vinaigrette:
  1½ cups olive oil
    1 cup safflower oil
   ¾ cup sherry vinegar
       juice of 1 lemon
    2 tablespoons sugar
    3 tablespoons prepared mustard
       salt and pepper to taste

Using shredding disc, process broccoli and blanche it in
boiling water for 2 minutes. Drain. Using julienne disc,
process other vegetables and mix together.

For vinaigrette, blend ingredients and toss with slaw.

Yield: 20 servings.

BROCCOLI SALAD WITH EGG CRESPELLE

  2½ pounds broccoli
    6 red bell peppers
   ½ cup dry white wine
   ½ cup cream
    1 cup olive oil
    2 garlic cloves, peeled
    2 tablespoons prepared mustard
    6 eggs, separated
   ⅓ cup all-purpose flour
    6 tablespoons grated Parmesan cheese
       freshly grated nutmeg
       butter and oil for pan

Cut broccoli into florets and stems into slices and blanch for 2 to 3 minutes. Drain and cool.

Halve and seed red peppers. Broil or place in 475°F oven for 10 minutes until skin blisters. Place in paper bag, twist closed, and let stand for a few minutes. Rub skin off and slice flesh into matchsticks.

Blend wine, cream, oil, garlic, and mustard in blender or processor. Toss salad, adding dressing slowly so that none pools on the bottom.

For egg pancakes, blend egg yolks, flour, and Parmesan cheese. Whisk egg whites with a touch of nutmeg and fold into yolks. Heat equal amounts of butter and oil to coat small omelet or crepe pan and place batter in pan, using a ¼-cup measure.

Cook like omelets, pulling batter back from sides for top to set. (You will have 4 or 5.)

Roll each pancake and let cool. Slice rolls on diagonal and gently fold into salad.

Yield: 20 servings.

CORN AND BARLEY SALAD

    4 cups cooked barley
    3 cups cooked corn kernels
    3 tablespoons snipped dill
    1 tablespoon chopped chives
 1½ cups olive oil
    ½ cup lemon juice
    ¼ teaspoon white pepper
    1 quart cherry tomatoes for garnish

Mix barley, corn, dill, and chives. Stir together olive oil, lemon juice, and pepper. Pour over salad and toss. Serve surrounded by cherry tomatoes.

Yield: 20 servings.

Buns, Muffins, etc.

SAFFRON BUNS

    1 cup milk
    ½ cup (1 stick) unsalted butter, melted
    1 teaspoon saffron threads, crumbled
    1 envelope active dry yeast dissolved in ¼-cup warm water
      and 2 tablespoons sugar
    4 cups unbleached all-purpose flour
    ½ teaspoon salt
    2 eggs, beaten
    ½ cup chopped candied orange peel
    ½ cup currants
    ½ cup chopped citron

Scald milk. Remove from heat and add butter and saffron, stirring to dissolve. Pour into large bowl and cool to lukewarm. Add yeast mixture. Incorporate flour and salt and turn blend onto floured board.

Knead for 5 minutes and place in greased bowl. Cover with clean towel and let rise 1 hour or until about double in bulk. Reserve about a half cup of dough.

Shape into 36 small round buns on greased baking sheet. Make small marbles of dough with reserved dough and top each bun with small sphere. Let rise one hour or more.

Bake at 350°F for 25 minutes or until golden.

Yield: 36.

PUMPKIN MUFFINS

2½ cups all-purpose flour
1¼ cups sugar
    pinch salt
1 tablespoon baking powder
1 teaspoon ground allspice
2 eggs, beaten
¼ cup (½ stick) unsalted butter, melted
¼ cup safflower oil
1 cup skim milk
1 can (16 ounces) solid-pack pumpkin
¾ cup chopped walnuts

Preheat oven to 400°F. Lightly grease and flour twenty ⅓-cup size muffin cups.

Mix flour, sugar, salt, baking powder, and allspice. Mix eggs, butter, oil, and milk. Combine with flour mixture and add pumpkin and nuts. Using a ¼-cup measure, fill prepared pan with batter. Put some water in any empty wells.

Bake for 20 minutes or until tester comes out clean.

Yield: 20.

MINIATURE SCONES

4 cups all-purpose flour
6 tablespoons sugar
1 tablespoon cream of tartar
2 teaspoons baking powder
¾ cup (1½ sticks) unsalted butter, diced
1½ cups milk
1 cup dried cherries or currants

Preheat oven to 425°F. Butter a baking sheet.

Combine flour, sugar, cream of tartar, and baking powder. Cut butter into flour mixture until it resembles corn meal. Stir in the milk until mixture forms a soft dough. Add dried cherries.

Roll or pat to ½-inch thickness and cut with a 1½-inch-round cutter. Place on prepared baking sheet. Bake for 10 minutes. Serve warm.

Yield: 20.

SMALL SAVORY CHEESE BISCUITS

  1 envelope active dry yeast
  1 tablespoon sugar
    large pinch salt
  ½ cup warm water
3½ cups all-purpose flour
  2 teaspoons baking powder
1½ cups milk
  ½ cup (1 stick) unsalted butter or margarine, melted
  6 ounces Monterey jack cheese with jalapeños, shredded
    (1½ cups)

Preheat oven to 425°F. Lightly butter and flour baking sheets.

Put yeast, sugar, and salt into warm water. Proof 10 minutes. Mix together flour and baking powder in a bowl large enough to hold all ingredients. In a separate bowl, mix milk and melted butter or margarine. Add yeast mixture and stir. Stir, then beat into flour with electric mixer at medium speed. Incorporate shredded cheese.

Knead slightly on floured surface and roll out to ½-inch thickness. Cut out biscuits with 1½-inch cutter and cover with a clean kitchen towel. Let rise for 1 hour or until doubled. Place on prepared baking sheets.

Bake for 20 minutes. Serve warm. They may be reheated.

Yield: 30.

PARMESAN-HERB BREADSTICKS

1 envelope active dry yeast
2 teaspoons sugar
½ teaspoon salt
1 cup warm water
3 cups all-purpose flour
½ cup olive oil
3 ounces Parmesan cheese, grated (¾ cup)
1 tablespoon mixed dried herbs

Proof yeast with sugar and salt in warm water and let stand 10 minutes.

Place flour in a large bowl and mix in oil and yeast mixture until blended. Add cheese and herbs, mixing until the batter is smooth and elastic. Cover and let rise about 1 hour or until doubled. (Dough will have a film of oil). Divide dough in half.

Preheat oven to 400°F. Lightly oil and flour baking sheets.

Roll first half dough on a floured surface to an ⅛-inch thickness. About 12 inches by 16 inches. Cut into strips a little under an inch wide and 6 inches long. Lift each strip. Fold in half and pull and twist till it is 6 inches again. Place on prepared baking sheets. Repeat with second half.

Bake 8 to 10 minutes until golden brown. Turn oven off and let sit another hour.

Yield: 72.

CORN-BREAD STICKS

½ cup diced sun-dried tomatoes
2 cups cornmeal
1½ cups all-purpose flour
½ teaspoon salt
1 tablespoon baking powder
4 eggs, beaten
2 cups buttermilk
5 tablespoons unsalted butter, melted
2 cups corn kernels

Preheat oven to 425°F. Grease corn-stick pans, place in oven, and let heat while oven preheats.

In a small bowl, pour boiling water over dried tomatoes. In another bowl, mix all dry ingredients. Beat eggs, milk, and butter until blended. Drain tomatoes.

Mix cornmeal mixture, tomatoes, and corn into beaten eggs just until blended. Fill prepared two-thirds pans.

Bake 20 minutes or until tester comes out clean. Cool slightly and unmold. Serve warm.

Yield: 20.

Soup

MINESTRONE

6 quarts beef or vegetable stock
12 ounces sun-dried tomato paste
2 cups diced fresh tomatoes
  pieces of crust from Parmesan cheese (optional)
  half of a lemon studded with cloves

1 whole onion
   sprigs fresh rosemary
2 cups diced onions
2 cups diced leeks
2 cups green peas
2 cups diced zucchini
2 cups diced celery
   salt and pepper to taste
2 cups cooked white beans
2 cups cooked chick-peas
3 cups uncooked tubetti or small elbow macaroni
8 ounces Parmesan cheese, grated (2 cups)
½ cup minced Italian (flat-leaf) parsley
2 cups diced potatoes

One way to make this is to combine all ingredients except grated Parmesan cheese and parsley and bring to a boil over low heat and simmer 45 minutes to 1 hour. Add Parmesan cheese and parsley just before serving.

Another way is to start boiling the broth using the stock, tomato paste, tomatoes, cheese rind, lemon, whole onion, and rosemary. Sauté onions and leeks, then potatoes, zucchini, and celery before adding to soup. Add salt and pepper, white beans, and chick-peas. Simmer 45 minutes. Add pasta and peas and cook another 15 minutes. Remove Parmesan crusts and add Parmesan cheese and parsley. Serve with garlic bread and additional grated Parmesan.

Yield: 24 servings.

CLAM CHOWDER

 ¾ cup (1½ sticks) unsalted butter
1½ cups diced onions
1½ cups diced celery
 1 cup all-purpose flour
 3 quarts clam broth
 1 tablespoon dried fines herbes
1½ quarts chopped clams
 6 cups boiled cubed potatoes
 1 quart milk
 1 quart cream
  paprika
  salt and pepper to taste

Melt butter in stockpot over medium heat. Add onions and celery and stir until transparent. Stir in flour until well blended. Add clam broth and herbes and simmer 20 minutes. Add clams and cooked potatoes.

 Lower heat so that clams do not boil and cook 5 minutes. Stir in milk and cream. Heat until chowder is quite hot, stirring so that it doesn't scorch. Serve sprinkled with paprika.

Yield: 20 servings.

ICED FRESH-TOMATO SOUP

20 tomatoes, peeled and seeded
 3 cucumbers, peeled and seeded
 5 quarts beef or vegetable stock
 4 garlic cloves, peeled
 1 4-inch piece gingerroot, peeled
 2 cups toasted bread cubes
  salt and pepper to taste

1 quart nonfat plain yogurt
  curry powder
1 pound cooked tiny Alaska shrimp for garnish
½ cup toasted sunflower seeds for garnish

Puree batches of tomatoes, cucumbers and 4 quarts stock in food processor. Process garlic, ginger, and bread cubes with 1 quart of broth and add to tomato puree. Add salt and pepper to taste and chill until ready to serve.

In a bowl, mix yogurt with curry powder to taste. In tureens for buffet or individual plates, ladle soup and top with curried yogurt. Garnish with shrimp and sunflower seeds.

Yield: 20 servings.

PUMPKIN SOUP

¼ cup (½ stick) unsalted butter
¼ cup safflower oil
4 leeks, cleaned and sliced
4 garlic cloves
2 pounds white mushrooms, stems and caps separated
4 pounds pureed fresh pumpkin (canned solid-pack may be substituted)
4 cinnamon sticks
2 teaspoons ground cumin
  salt and pepper to taste
5 quarts chicken or vegetable stock
2 cups sherry (optional)
3 cups heavy cream
2 cups salsa
  heavy cream and salsa for garnish

In skillet with butter and oil, brown leeks, garlic, and mushroom stems. Lift out with slotted spoon and reserve. Slice mushroom caps, sauté, and reserve.

In stockpot, cook pumpkin with reserved leeks mixture, cinnamon sticks, cumin, and salt and pepper in stock until quite tender, about 1 hour. Remove cinnamon sticks, cool slightly, and puree in batches, then return to pot with sliced mushrooms and sherry. Heat to serve.

May be refrigerated and heated when needed. Serve with swirls of heavy cream and a touch of salsa to taste.

Yield: 20 servings.

DEEP-GREEN SPLIT PEA SOUP

        6 quarts water or stock
          ham bone (optional)
     1½ pounds green split peas
        1 bunch parsley, minced
        3 pounds spinach, chopped
        6 carrots, scraped and diced
        6 stalks celery, strings removed and diced
        2 onions, diced
        1 onion stuck with 10 whole cloves
          several sprigs fresh thyme or 2 teaspoons dried
        2 jalapeño peppers, seeded and diced (optional)
          salt and pepper to taste
          fresh croutons (recipe, page 169) for garnish

Rinse split peas and pick over. If ham bone is used, place in cold water and bring to a boil. Remove at the end of the cooking process.

Or bring water or stock to a boil and add all ingredients. Bring to a boil, stirring frequently. Lower heat, continue stirring, and cook until peas are tender, about 1½ hours. If soup gets too thick at any point, add some water or stock. Garnish with croutons, freshly made, if possible.

Yield: 20 servings.

Pasta, etc.

COLD SESAME NOODLES

2 pounds short flat Chinese noodles
¼ cup sesame oil

Sauce:
8 tablespoons Chinese sesame paste
liquid from sesame paste jar
1½ cups low-sodium soy sauce
¾ cup honey
⅓ cup sesame oil
2 tablespoons hot chili oil

Optional Toppings—one or all may be used:
1 large cucumber, peeled, seeded, and cubed
1 cup roasted peanuts, chopped
½ cup toasted sesame seeds
½ pound preserved tofu, cubed
½ cup Chinese or Italian (flat-leaf) parsley
½ cup minced scallions

Boil noodles according to package directions. Drain and run under cold water, drain again, and coat with ¼ cup sesame oil. Cover and refrigerate.

Combine all ingredients for sauce using immersion blender or mixer on slow. Use less hot oil if you are timid about the spice. If sauce is too hot, add more honey and sesame paste. Cover and store until ready to use. Will keep several days but must be stirred again and may need 1 to 2 tablespoons boiling water.

Toss with noodles. Add toppings just before serving.

Yield: 20 servings.

CLASSIC BOSTON BAKED BEANS

    2 pounds small white or brown beans
    6 quarts water
    2 cups chopped onion
    1 cup honey
    1 cup molasses
    ½ cup bourbon
    ½ cup packed brown sugar
    1 cup cider vinegar
    2 tablespoons dry mustard
    1 pound salt pork, cubed (optional)

Soak beans overnight and cook for 1 hour or until tender. Drain and mix with other ingredients. Place in covered baking dish or special bean crock and bake at 300°F for 2 hours, stirring occasionally. Remove cover and bake another 30 minutes.

Yield: 20 servings.

SPAGHETTI WITH RICH TOMATO-MUSHROOM SAUCE

    6 pork chops
    3 onions, diced
    4 celery stalks, diced
    4 carrots, scraped and diced
    3 pounds white mushrooms

½ cup olive oil

8 pounds tomatoes, crushed, peeled and seeded (four 30-oz cans may be substituted)

10 ounces tomato paste (four 2½-oz cans)

2 heads garlic

2 cups basil leaves

1 cup Italian flat-leaf parsley

2 cups dry red wine

1 lemon, seeded and cut into quarters

½ cup sugar

2 tablespoons dried oregano, crumbled

4 pounds spaghetti, freshly cooked until al dente and drained

   freshly grated Parmesan cheese

Brown pork chops in large heavy saucepan. Add onions, celery, and carrots and cook, stirring, until slightly browned. Stir in mushrooms. Add olive oil as needed. Add remaining ingredients except spaghetti and cheese and cook for 3 hours on low heat, stirring occasionally. Sauce will be thick. Wine or water splashed with balsamic vinegar may be added (up to two cups) if necessary.

   Serve over spaghetti and top with freshly grated Parmesan cheese.

Yield: 20 servings.

SAFFRON RISOTTO

- 4 cups dried mushrooms (weight varies)
- 3 quarts turkey or chicken stock, preferably unsalted
- 3 cups dry white wine
- 4 onions, diced
- ¼ cup olive oil
- 6 cups Arborio rice
- 1 teaspoon crumbled saffron threads in ¼ cup hot water
- 4 ounces Parmesan cheese, grated (1 cup)
- 5 tablespoons unsalted butter
  freshly ground pepper to taste

Pour boiling water over dried mushrooms just to cover.
Set aside. In a stockpot, bring stock to a boil, add
wine, and simmer as risotto is being made. In a large
heavy-bottomed casserole over medium heat, cook onions
in olive oil until transparent. Add the rice 1 cup at a
time, stirring until the grains are coated, about 4 minutes.
Do not brown onions or rice.

Add 2 cups of simmering broth to risotto and stir
continuously. As liquid is absorbed, add 1 or 2 cups at a
time, stirring gently. After 15 minutes, start adding
undrained mushrooms and incorporate.

Add half of the saffron mixture and more liquid.
Total cooking time is about 30 minutes. After 25 minutes
taste a grain and see if it is cooked through. Add
remaining saffron. All liquid may not be needed, but if
more is needed add water. When grains are cooked
through but al dente, remove from heat and stir in grated
Parmesan. Serve immediately.

Yield: 20 servings.

SAFFRON NOODLES

1 teaspoon saffron threads, crumbled
2 cups (4 sticks) unsalted butter
   salt and freshly ground pepper to taste
4 pounds flat egg noodles, freshly cooked until just past al
   dente and drained

Stir crushed saffron in ¼ cup hot water and let stand for
15 minutes.

Melt butter and incorporate saffron in liquid, the salt,
and pepper. Toss with noodles.

Note: The addition of chicken livers and roasted red
peppers sautéed with chives and wine turns this into a
main dish for lunch or buffets.

Yield: 20 servings.

BAKED ZITI WITH FOUR CHEESES

4 pounds uncooked ziti
⅓ cup olive oil
2 cups dry white wine
3 pounds fresh ricotta cheese
1 pound mozzarella cheese, shredded (4 cups)
1 pound mozzarella cheese, thinly sliced
1 pound fontina cheese, shredded
8 ounces Parmesan cheese, grated (2 cups)
1 quart milk
½ cup chopped basil leaves
   salt and freshly ground pepper to taste
1 tablespoon freshly grated nutmeg

Preheat oven to 350°F.

Boil ziti in 10 quarts of water until al dente. Drain.
Return to pot and toss with oil and wine.

Reserve sliced mozzarella and 1 cup grated Parmesan for topping and stir in all other ingredients until evenly mixed.

Turn into a 10-quart roasting pan or two smaller pans. Top with remaining mozzarella and Parmesan.

Bake for 30 minutes until lightly browned and bubbly.

Note: Sun-dried tomatoes in oil or minced pancetta or prosciutto ends may be added to mixture before baking.

Yield: 20 servings.

ROLAND PARK FOOLPROOF PIZZA

    1 envelope active dry yeast
    ¼ cup warm water
    1 teaspoon sugar
    2 cups all-purpose flour
    ½ teaspoon salt
    ½ cup cold water
    ¼ cup olive oil
      cornmeal for pan
    ½ cup tomato paste
    2 tablespoons olive oil
    ½ teaspoon dried oregano
    ¾ cup thinly sliced mushrooms
   10 ounces mozzarella cheese shredded (2½ cups)

In medium-size bowl, proof yeast in ¼ cup warm water with sugar for 10 minutes or until yeast mixture bubbles. Add flour, salt, cold water, and ¼ cup olive oil. Mix thoroughly and knead by hand 4 minutes, adding up to

½ cup additional flour until dough is spongy but not sticky.

Set dough in oiled bowl and cover. Place in a warm, draft-free place and let rise at least 45 minutes and up to 1½ hours.

When dough has approximately doubled in size it is ready to roll out for baking. Once it rises it will be a little sticky, which is what makes it crisp in a home oven.

Preheat oven to 450°F. Place stone in oven if one is being used.

On a flour-dusted surface using dusted rolling pin, roll pizza to size of 16 × 20-inch sheet pan or stone, curling up a ¾-inch border.

Sprinkle medium-ground cornmeal on lightly oiled baking sheet before laying dough on or place dough directly on stone.

Bake for 7 minutes. Remove from hot oven and spread with tomato paste and drizzle 2 tablespoons olive oil. Sprinkle with oregano and mushrooms. Top with shredded mozzarella.

Return to hot oven and bake 8 to 10 minutes longer. Using pizza cutter or chef's knife, cut into 4-inch squares, leaving gaps to allow moisture to escape. Serve with crushed red pepper.

Yield: 20 servings.

POSOLE, NEW MEXICAN STYLE

Posole is blue or yellow dry hominy with the parchment skin in place. Uncooked posole must be soaked in three quarts of water for 12 to 15 hours. Do not substitute traditional hominy.

2½ pounds posole
5 pounds boneless chicken thighs
2 large Spanish onions, (1 pound)
8 dried chile pepper pods
2 heads garlic
2 pounds sweet potatoes
2 pounds carrots, scraped
5 cinnamon sticks
6 twigs of epazote (optional)
2 teaspoons ground cinnamon
½ teaspoon ground mace
1 tablespoon dried oregano
   olive oil
6 tablespoons tomato paste
1 quart beer
   salt and pepper to taste
3 large ripe avocados
2 large ripe papayas
   sour cream
   lime slices and chopped cilantro for garnish
   Fried Plantain Chips (recipe, page 191)

After posole has been soaked, rinse it and set to boil in large covered stockpot. Lower heat and simmer for 3 hours or until kernels pop and open. Check every half hour or so and add water only if needed. Taste a grain of the posole to make sure the texture is soft and chewy.

In Dutch oven or comparable pot, set chicken thighs, cut in 2 or 3 pieces, and place in large skillet over moderate heat. When they start to sizzle, place onions and peppers in pan. Peel garlic cloves, dice sweet potatoes, and julienne carrots. Add to chicken with spices and stir. Keep on low heat for about 20 minutes, adding olive oil as needed to keep from sticking.

Add chicken and vegetables to posole and stir in tomato paste and beer. Add salt and pepper to taste and cook on low heat for another 30 minutes. Remove whole chiles and cinnamon sticks.

Cover the pot and let it stand up to 30 minutes. Serve topped with diced avocado and papaya and sour cream and garnish with slices of lime and chopped cilantro. Accompany with Fried Plantain Chips.

Yield: 20 servings.

FRIED PLANTAIN CHIPS

  4 green plantains, sliced 1/16-inch thick with processor
     oil for deep frying
½ teaspoon coarse (kosher) salt
1 tablespoon brown sugar
½ teaspoon cayenne pepper
½ teaspoon ground cinnamon

Fry plantain slices and drain well on paper towels. Sprinkle with a mixture of salt, sugar, cayenne, and cinnamon.

Yield: 6 cups.

Fish and Shellfish

WHOLE POACHED SALMON

>One 10-pound salmon, cleaned and scaled
>cheesecloth to wrap fish twice
>
>2 quarts water
>2 cups dry white wine
>2 strips lemon peel
>3 sprigs fresh parsley
>¼ cup chopped celery
>1 onion stuck with several cloves
>2 bay leaves
>Sauce Mousseline (recipe, page 193)
>Cucumber-Dill Dressing (recipe, page 194)
>cucumber slices, and cooked string beans for garnish

Dampen cheesecloth and wring out. Wrap salmon in at least 2 turns of cheesecloth in such a way that it will be easy to remove. It will probably be necessary to remove the head of the fish so that it comfortably fits the poacher.

Remove rack from poacher and place remaining ingredients except garnishes in poacher and bring to a boil over two burners on top of the stove. Lower heat and simmer for 15 minutes. Set salmon on poaching rack.

Carefully lower fish into simmering water which should cover fish. Cover poacher and gently bring back to a simmer and time for 10 minutes an inch of the fish at the thickest part, until water actively simmers again.

From the point it starts to simmer in the bouillon it will be approximately 45 minutes for this large a fish.

Lift out fish on its rack and place on a tray which has been covered with foil-covered cardboard. Take off the cheesecloth using a sharp knife or scissors to cut the cloth where it sticks and gently slide it out from under the fish.

Usually the salmon is served flat and only the top skin is discarded. Remove fins and any small bones with your fingers or a pair of tweezers. Scrape brown flesh where visible to show only a pink surface. Cover with plastic wrap and chill in the refrigerator for several hours or overnight.

Sauce Mousseline is an optional sauce to coat and garnish the fish. If it is being used this way, place it on the salmon one hour before serving so that the platter can be returned to the refrigerator for the sauce to set in place.

When ready to serve, remove wrap and gently slide onto serving platter.

Yield: 20 servings.

SAUCE MOUSSELINE

  6 egg yolks
    pinch each salt, pepper, and grated nutmeg
  1 cup (2 sticks) unsalted butter, cut in thin slices
  1 cup heavy cream, whipped until stiff peaks form

In the top of a double boiler set over 2 inches of hot, not boiling water, whisk egg yolks with salt, pepper, and nutmeg. Gradually incorporate butter and stir until thick. Remove from heat and cool.

When yolk mixture is thoroughly cooled, fold into whipped cream. Spread a thin layer on the cold salmon and refrigerate, reserving excess sauce. Shortly before serving, add another layer of mousseline and return to refrigerator.

Decorate with cucumber slices to resemble fish scales or use strips of cooked string beans placed in half circles to outline scales.

Yield: 1 quart.

CUCUMBER-DILL DRESSING

    4 cucumbers
    ½ cup cider vinegar
    ½ cup water
    ½ cup sugar
    1 cup bottled horseradish
    2 cups nonfat plain yogurt
    ½ cup minced fresh dill

Peel cucumber, cut in half lengthwise, seed, and slice ¼-inch thick. Place in colander, sprinkle with salt, and let drain for 30 minutes. Rinse and blend with remaining ingredients and chill until serving time. If desired, salt and pepper to taste.

Yield: 1 quart.

SALMON BURGERS

    5 pounds cooked salmon
      whites from 5 eggs
    1 cup grated red onion
    1½ cups salsa
    3 tablespoons minced drained capers
    3 cups fresh corn-bread crumbs
      juice of 2 lemons
      freshly ground pepper to taste
      safflower oil

Flake salmon. Whip egg whites until opaque and foamy but not stiff. Mix all ingredients except oil and shape into 20 patties about ¾-inch thick. Sauté on griddle or in large skillet brushed heavily with safflower oil until lightly golden on both sides.

Yield: 20.

CRANBERRY KETCHUP

- 1 pound cranberries
- ⅓ cup white vinegar
- ¾ cup sugar
- 2 cinnamon sticks
- 2 teaspoons ground allspice
  salt and pepper to taste
  red pepper flakes to taste (optional)

Cover cranberries with water in medium saucepan and bring to boil. Remove from heat, cool, and drain. Place in food processor for 5 to 10 seconds depending on power.

Return to saucepan with remaining ingredients and cook over low heat for 20 minutes.

Yield: 1 pint.

BAKED SALMON FILLETS ON ROASTED TOMATOES

    5 pounds fresh firm tomatoes
    1 head garlic
    ½ cup olive oil
    2 cups dry white wine
    1 tablespoon dried thyme
    1 teaspoon ground cumin
       freshly ground pepper
       twenty 6- or 7-ounce salmon fillets
    ¾ olive oil
       Saffron Noodles (recipe, page 187)

Preheat oven to 500°F. Peel tomatoes, cut in half, and seed. Peel and separate cloves of garlic. Place tomatoes and garlic in single layer in roasting pans and drizzle with the ½ cup olive oil. Roast for 10 minutes.

Mix wine with thyme, cumin, and pepper and pour into pans. Lay salmon in single layer over tomatoes and drizzle the ¾ cup olive oil over fish. Lower oven temperature to 400°F.

Bake for 15 minutes or until fish is firm and no longer transparent. Serve with Saffron Noodles.

Yield: 20 servings.

SWEET AND SOUR FISH

    5 pounds scrod or pollock, cut into 1-inch cubes
    1½ cups "instant flour"
    1½ cups chestnut flour or cornstarch
       saffflower oil
    1 large or 2 medium pineapples, cut in ¾-inch cubes
    8 large firm tomatoes, each cut in 8 wedges
    ¼ cup sugar

¾ cup cider vinegar
½ cup sherry
½ cup low-sodium soy sauce
1 cup ginger marmalade
1½ cups water

Lightly dredge the fish in a mixture of flour and chestnut flour or cornstarch. Heat oil in large skillet. Sauté fish in batches for 4 or 5 minutes. Remove to a warm platter or nonreactive ovenproof dish. Drain any excess oil from skillet and add pineapples and tomatoes. Stir for several minutes and pour remaining ingredients into pan, stir, and cook for 10 minutes until heated through and pour over fish. Accompany with rice.

Yield: 20 servings.

SCALLOPS WITH ANGEL HAIR PASTA IN LEMON CREAM SAUCE

Lemon Cream Sauce:
4 pounds small scallops (sliced if large)
2 cups finely ground bread crumbs
1 cup all-purpose flour
½ cup (1 stick) unsalted butter
½ cup olive oil
  juice and zest of 4 lemons
2 cups minced shallots
2 tablespoons sugar
4 cups dry white wine
1 quart skim milk
1 quart cream
3½ pounds spinach fettuccine, freshly cooked and drained
1 cup chopped fresh parsley leaves
  freshly grated lemon zest, nutmeg, and pepper

Slice scallops, if large. Combine bread crumbs and flour. Dredge scallops in bread crumbs and flour. Reserve excess mixture. Heat butter and oil in stainless pan and sauté scallops and lemon zest over low heat. Remove and keep warm.

Add shallots to oil in pan, adding more butter and oil if necessary. Wilt, but do not brown. Stir and add lemon juice and sugar. Stir in reserved flour mixture. Incorporate wine and milk and cook for 15 minutes, stirring occasionally. Add cream and cook 5 minutes longer. Add scallops.

Serve plated fettuccine and sauce topped with chopped parsley and additional lemon zest and grated nutmeg and pepper.

Yield: 20 servings.

TUNA MEDALLIONS

Twenty 6-ounce tuna steaks (each 2 inches thick)
¾ cup olive oil
⅓ cup prepared mustard
⅓ cup lemon juice
1 teaspoon cracked black pepper
Cubed Potatoes (recipe, page 199)
zucchini

Brush both sides of tuna steaks with a mixture of oil, mustard, lemon juice, and pepper. Broil under flame or on top of stove broiler, 4 minutes per side or to taste. Serve with Cubed Potatoes and steamed green and yellow zucchini, if desired.

Yield: 20 servings.

CUBED POTATOES

10 baking potatoes
    paprika
40 small shallots
40 whole cloves
⅓ cup olive oil
4 or 5 sprigs fresh rosemary
    coarse (kosher) salt

Peel potatoes and cut into ½-inch cubes, drop into ice water, drain, and dry. Sprinkle potatoes with paprika. Peel shallots and insert clove in each.

    Heat a shallow layer of oil with rosemary sprigs in skillet. Add shallots and potatoes and cook until brown and tender. Drain on paper towels and serve sprinkled with coarse salt.

Yield: 20 servings.

PAN-ROASTED RED SNAPPER

2 cups chopped red onion
2 cups chopped yellow pepper
1 teaspoon ground cumin
1 teaspoon red pepper flakes
2½ cups chopped cilantro or parsley leaves
1 cup olive oil
1½ cups pimiento-stuffed Spanish olives
6½ pounds red snapper fillets
1 cup orange juice
½ cup lemon juice
½ cup lime juice
    olives and chopped parsley for garnish
    Andean Potatoes (recipe, page 200)

Preheat oven to 400°F. Add onions and peppers to ½ cup of the olive oil in skillet. Cook, stirring until wilted. Coat roasting pan with remaining oil and set fish on it. Roast for 10 minutes.

Add juices to oil mixture in skillet and pour over fish. Bake 10 minutes longer until fish flakes easily.

Garnish with olives and chopped parsley. Serve with Andean Potatoes.

Yield: 20 servings.

ANDEAN POTATOES

  4 pounds potatoes, boiled and mashed
  1 teaspoon chili powder
  1 cup cream
  1 cup plain yogurt
  ½ cup lemon juice
  6 ounces white Cheddar cheese, shredded (1½ cups)

Mash potatoes, gradually incorporating all ingredients.

Yield: 20 servings.

REGIONAL BOUILLABAISSE

1½ gallons water
  1 head fennel
  1 head celery, 6 inches from root portion
    large Spanish onion
  4 leeks
  ¼ cup minced basil leaves
  8 tomatoes
20 small red potatoes, quartered
  6 tablespoons tomato paste

2 teaspoons crushed saffron
  grated rind of 1 orange
3 small bluefish
6 whitings
1 weakfish
2 pounds clams
2 pounds mussels
½ cup Pernod or other anise-flavored liqueur
½ cup minced parsley leaves

Bring water to a boil with a little salt and pepper in a nonreactive saucepan. Dice fennel, celery, onions, leeks, and basil. Peel, seed, and dice tomatoes. Add diced vegetables to pot. Cook 30 minutes.

Add potatoes, tomato paste, saffron, and orange rind. Gently boil for another 15 minutes.

Clean all fish and discard skin and bones. Shell shellfish. Lower heat so that stock is simmering and add fish.

Cook for 8 minutes and add shellfish. Cook another 4 minutes and remove from heat. Stir in Pernod and parsley. Serve with garlic bread.

Yield: 20 servings.

GUMBO

¼ cup (½ stick) unsalted butter
¾ cup all-purpose flour
5 slices bacon, diced (optional)
½ cup olive oil
1 cup *each* diced onion, celery, carrot, and green pepper
4 quarts fish stock or 3 quarts water
2 pints clam juice
2 tablespoons tomato paste
1 teaspoon dried oregano
1 teaspoon dried thyme
5 bay leaves
¼ teaspoon white pepper
¼ teaspoon black pepper
¼ teaspoon cayenne or to taste
2 pounds andouille sausage, sliced
2 pounds small uniform okra, rinsed, dried, and cut in half
    lengthwise
2 pounds shrimp, shelled and deveined
3 pounds crabmeat
3 pounds peeled diced fresh tomatoes
Plain White Rice (recipe, page 203)

Melt butter in a heavy iron Dutch oven or comparable heavy pan over medium heat. To make roux: Add ¼ cup of the flour and stir until incorporated. Add diced bacon and stir until brown but not crisp. Add ¼ cup of oil, stir, and add another ¼ cup of flour, blending well. Add remaining oil and flour, and stir. Add 1 pint of liquid and stir until incorporated and mixture is thick.

Add liquid pint by pint, stirring continuously. Bring to boil. Add diced vegetables, tomato paste, herbs and seasonings.

Add sausage and okra. Cook 20 minutes or until okra is just tender. Add shrimp and stir for 3 or 4 minutes.

Add crabmeat and cook and stir for 5 minutes.
Remove from heat and stir in tomato. Serve with Plain
White Rice.

Yield: 20 servings.

PLAIN WHITE RICE

2 pounds southern white rice
3 quarts boiling water
   lemon, quartered and seeded
6 fish bouillon cubes (optional)

Stir rice into boiling water in a large pot. Add lemon and
bouillon cubes. Cover, lower heat, and simmer 20
minutes.

Remove from heat. Lift lid, set clean towel across top
of pot, and replace lid over it. Let stand 5 minutes. Stir
with slotted spoon and serve.

Yield: 20 servings.

SALMON STEAKS

20 salmon steaks (6 or 8 ounces each)
   safflower oil for brushing steaks
   juice of 4 lemons
   Onion Jam (recipe, page 204)

Preheat grill. For a main dish, serve fish steak whole, and
for an appetizer or buffet, cut in half and remove bone.

Brush steaks with oil and sprinkle with lemon juice.
Broil 5 minutes. Turn and broil 5 minutes or until meat
is no longer translucent when tested near the bone. Serve
with Onion Jam.

Yield: 20 main-dish servings or 40 appetizer servings.

ONION JAM

  1 cup dried cherries
 20 onions (medium-large)
 ¼ cup (½ stick) unsalted butter
 ¼ cup olive oil
 ¼ cup sugar
  2 cups dry red or white wine
  1 cup crème de cassis

Pour ¾ cup boiling water over cherries and let stand 15 minutes.

Peel and slice onions, separating rings.

In a large sauté pan, warm butter and oil over moderate heat. Sauté onions until transparent. Add sugar and stir. Lower heat and stir in wine and crème de cassis.

Add cherries to pan, stirring until all the liquid has been absorbed.

Yield: 20 servings.

TANGY HALIBUT

 ¾ ounces unsalted butter
 ¾ ounces olive oil
    twenty 8-ounce halibut steaks
  3 lemons, sliced paper thin
    Quick Tapenade (recipe, page 205)
    Piquant Sweet Potatoes (recipe, page 205)

Preheat oven to 400°F. Melt butter and mix with olive oil and place half in roasting pans.

Put fish flat in pans and drizzle remaining butter and oil over fish and lay lemon slices on the top.

Roast for 15 minutes or until fish is no longer transparent. Lift fish with slotted spatula.

Serve with Quick Tapenade. Accompany with Piquant Sweet Potatoes.

Yield: 20 servings.

QUICK TAPENADE

½ cup olive oil
5 garlic cloves, sliced
2 cans flat anchovies, drained
2 tablespoons salted capers, well rinsed
1 jar (7 ounce) olive paste
  juice of 1 lemon
¼ cup cognac

Heat olive oil in saucepan and add garlic. Cook until wilted. Add anchovies and capers, stirring until anchovies are almost dissolved. Stir in olive paste, lemon juice, and cognac. Cook until heated through and plate with halibut.

Yield: 2½ cups.

PIQUANT SWEET POTATOES

1 cup (2 sticks) unsalted butter
1 cup packed brown sugar
8 pounds cooked sweet potatoes
2 pounds tomatoes, peeled, seeded, and diced
½ cup chopped, peeled shallots
3 tablespoons drained, chopped preserved serrano chili

Heat oven to 350°F. Heat butter and brown sugar in roasting pan until butter is melted. Stir in remaining ingredients. Cut potatoes in large cubes. Bake 25 minutes or until browned.

Yield: 20 servings.

Poultry and Meat

SZECHUAN CHICKEN BREASTS

  5 pounds boneless, skinless chicken breasts
  3 large green peppers
  1½ pounds white button mushrooms
  4 bunches scallions
     peanut oil
  1 tablespoon aniseed
  1 tablespoon ground ginger
  ½ cup packed brown sugar
  2 tablespoons ground Szechuan peppercorns
  2 cups raw unsalted peanuts or cashews
  3 cups chicken broth
  2 cups low-sodium soy sauce
  1 cup sherry

Cut chicken into strips. Seed and julienne peppers and slice mushrooms thickly. Trim scallions of roots and tough green part. Slice lengthwise into quarters.

It is probably necessary to do this divided in two batches. Heat peanut oil in two large woks or skillets with aniseed, ginger, sugar, and ground peppercorns over high heat. Add chicken, pepper, mushrooms, scallions, and nuts evenly to each. Cook, stirring, for 7 minutes or until chicken is opaque and firm. Lower heat and add broth, soy sauce, and sherry. Simmer for 10 minutes.

Yield: 20 servings.

CHICKEN BREASTS STUFFED WITH CHÈVRE AND SUN-DRIED TOMATOES

  2 pounds crumbly chèvre
  5 ounces olive paste
  1 cup diced sun-dried tomatoes in oil
20 boneless chicken breast halves with skin on
     olive oil
     paprika
     Tomato Coulis (recipe, page 208)
     Polenta Squares (recipe, page 207)

Preheat oven to 450°F. Set out pans large enough to hold chicken in single layer.

Mix together cheese, olive paste, and sun-dried tomatoes. Gently lift skin and put 2 tablespoons filling between chicken and skin. Smooth skin to cover filling.

Oil pans and place chicken in one layer. Drizzle oil over chicken and sprinkle with paprika.

Bake for 12 to 15 minutes. Plate each chicken breast on Tomato Coulis with a side-dish of two Polenta Squares.

Yield: 20 servings.

POLENTA SQUARES

  3 quarts water
  4 cups polenta
  2 teaspoons coarse (kosher) salt
  1 cup (2 sticks) unsalted butter
     olive oil

Bring water to a boil with salt. Pour in polenta, stirring continuously. Cook 20 minutes, stirring frequently.

Remove from heat and stir in butter.

Serve immediately or pour into two 16 × 20-inch pans and let set. Cut into 4-inch squares. Lightly brush with olive oil and broil for 2 to 3 minutes until top is crisp and lightly browned.

Yield: 40.

TOMATO COULIS

    3 tablespoons olive oil
    2 red onions, diced
    6 garlic cloves, peeled
    1 can (#35) tomato puree
    2 ounces tomato paste
    ⅓ cup balsamic vinegar
    2 tablespoons sugar
      coarse (kosher) salt and freshly ground pepper to taste
    2 pounds ripe tomatoes
      basil leaves for garnish

Put all ingredients except ripe tomatoes and basil leaves in food processor and pulse until smooth. Pour into bowl. If coulis seems too thin, thicken with up to ½ cup bread crumbs and ¼ cup grated Parmesan cheese.

Peel, seed, and dice tomatoes and mix into sauce. Garnish with basil.

Yield: 5 cups.

CRISP DUCK À L'ORANGE

     5 whole ducks with giblets
    12 seedless oranges
       sprigs of fresh thyme
     1 onion
    10 whole cloves

6 bay leaves
1 teaspoon ground mace
2 cups shallots, peeled
2 tablespoons unsalted butter
2 tablespoons olive oil
1 cup Triple Sec or other orange liqueur

Preheat oven to 400°F. Clean and dry ducks and remove and reserve giblets. Cut up 5 of the oranges and place one in cavity of each duck with a sprig of thyme. Pierce skin in several places and place ducks on rack over roasting pan and roast for 30 minutes until a good deal of fat has dripped into pan.

While ducks are roasting, set 2 quarts of water to boil with a little salt and pepper. Peel onion and insert cloves, then place in water with bay leaves, mace, thyme, and giblets except for livers. Cook giblets 20 minutes.

Grate the zest of 5 oranges. Place in small saucepan, cover with water, bring to boil, lower flame, and set aside.

Sauté duck livers and minced shallots in butter and olive oil. When liver is cooked, remove from heat and dice.

Remove giblets from simmering water and dice. Continue simmering water to reduce.

In blender or processor, place orange rind and its cooking water, liver, shallots, and giblets. Place in medium saucepan with triple sec and 4 cups of giblet stock. Stir sauce until ready to serve. Adjust flavor before plating.

Discard all fat from ducks in the oven and reset on racks over roasting pans. Squeeze juice of 1 orange over each duck and place thinly sliced oranges over all. Lower heat to 325°F and roast for another hour.

Test for doneness. See if drumstick moves easily and meat pulls from bone.

Present on platter garnished with orange slices and sauce in sauciers, or plate individually serving a few slices of meat with an occasional drumstick. Discard the tip of the wing and serve the joint with the single bone.

Yield: 20 servings.

TURKEY CHILI MOLE

safflower oil to start cooking
3 large onions diced
1 large head garlic, cloves peeled
5 assorted chiles (ancho, cascabel, etc.)
4 ounces best-quality chili powder
7 pounds ground turkey
1 can (#10) crushed tomatoes
2 cans (#2½) tomato paste
1 tablespoon ground cinnamon
½ teaspoon ground cloves
2 teaspoons ground cumin
1½ teaspoons black pepper
8 ounces bittersweet chocolate, broken up
up to 1 quart water or stock, if necessary

In a 7-quart stew pot, place enough oil to wilt onions and start cooking garlic. Mince chiles and add with chili powder and stir. Gradually add ground turkey and crushed tomatoes. Stir in tomato paste, cinnamon, cloves, cumin, and pepper. Stir frequently as chili starts to simmer. Add chocolate.

Stir and cook for 1½ hours until chili is dark and thick. Add water or stock only if it starts sticking.

Serve with yellow rice mixed with pine nuts, raisins, and sliced pimiento-stuffed Spanish olives, if you wish.

Yield: 20 servings.

BEEF CURRY

1 quart nonfat plain yogurt
4 tablespoons quality curry powder
1 tablespoon ground cumin
2 teaspoons crushed red pepper (optional or to taste)
1 4-inch piece gingerroot, peeled
1 tablespoon ground cardamom
8 pounds boneless sirloin, cut in 2-inch cubes
  all-purpose flour to coat
4 large onions, sliced
2 cup ghee or mixture of butter and oil
2 pounds button mushrooms, sliced
5 large unpeeled apples, sliced
  up to 1 quart apple juice as needed
  chopped cilantro leaves and whole cloves for garnish

In processor, blend yogurt, curry powder, cumin, red pepper, gingerroot, and cardamom. Set out a large Dutch oven or stew pot. Dredge beef in flour.

In a large skillet, brown beef and onions in a single layer, adding more ghee or butter mixture as needed. Transfer browned beef to stew pot. Sauté apple slices in same skillet and add to pot. Set over medium heat. Stir in yogurt-spice blend and mushrooms. Cook for 1 hour.

If mixture gets dry, add up to 1 quart apple juice, a cup at a time. Accompany with rice and peach chutney.

Serve rice in a dome made by filling a lightly oiled

bowl with rice and gently unmolding it. Circle with chopped cilantro and stud with whole cloves.

Yield: 20 servings.

PEACH CHUTNEY

10 pounds peaches, halved and pitted
 8 ounces raisins
 3 large Spanish onions, diced
 5 lemons, seeded and diced, peel and all
 2 tablespoons crushed red pepper (this will be quite hot, use to taste)
 1 tablespoon dry mustard
 2 cups granulated sugar
 2 cups packed brown sugar
 4 to 6 short cinnamon sticks
   cider vinegar to cover

Cut each peach half into about 8 pieces and mince raisins. Place in nonreactive stockpot over medium heat. Add remaining ingredients and stir until it starts to boil. Lower heat and simmer, stirring frequently, for 2 hours.

If it is going to be used within a few weeks, wash hinged preserving jars with rubber gasket in hot soapy water, rinse thoroughly, and keep under refrigeration.

Yield: 2 quarts.

FILET MIGNON ROAST WITH MADEIRA SAUCE

   Two 6-pound beef roasts (will trim to 5 pounds each)
¾ cup prepared mustard
   freshly ground black pepper
   Madeira Sauce (recipe, page 213)

Rub trimmed roasts with mustard and a touch of pepper. Set on rack over roasting pan. Put in oven no more than 45 minutes before it is to be eaten.

Preheat oven to 425°F. Place roasts in hot oven for 15 minutes, then lower oven temperature to 400°F and roast for 20 minutes or until meat thermometer registers 140°F (medium rare).

Cut parallel to the grain and plate with Madeira Sauce. Accompany with asparagus and potatoes.

Yield: 20 servings.

MADEIRA SAUCE

- 2 pounds small white mushrooms
- ¾ cup shallots, peeled and minced
- 1 cup (2 sticks) butter
- ¾ red currant jelly
- ¼ cup (½ stick) unsalted butter
- ½ cup "instant" flour
- 3 cups beef stock or unsalted beef bouillon
- ⅓ cup minced parsley leaves
- 1 cup Madeira wine
- salt and pepper to taste

In a sauté pan, brown mushrooms and shallots in the 1 cup butter. Stir in red currant jelly until dissolved. Keep warm.

In a medium saucepan over low heat, make a brown roux by melting the ¼ cup butter and then whisk in flour. Gradually add beef stock and Madeira. Reduce slightly. Add reserved mushrooms and stir. Serve with filets.

Yield: 1 quart.

NATURALLY CURED HAM

      One 16 to 17-pound naturally cured Polish-style ham
  2 cups peach chutney
  ½ cup prepared mustard
  25 whole cloves

Preheat oven to 375°F. Remove rind from ham and trim fat to ⅛ inch. Score checkerboard pattern into fat. Puree chutney and mustard and coat ham. Set a clove in the center of each square. Bake for 30 minutes. Lower heat and continue roasting for 1 hour.

      Remove to platter and garnish with chutney and cinnamon sticks. Serve with Wild Rice and Mushrooms.

Yield: 20 servings.

WILD RICE AND MUSHROOMS

  4 quarts boiling water
  2 cups dried mushrooms, crumbled into chunky pieces
  4½ cups wild rice
  1 cup shallots, peeled
      salt and pepper to taste

Pour 2 cups of boiling water over mushrooms in small bowl and set aside.

      Add rice to boiling water over moderate heat with shallots and a touch of salt and pepper. Cover and cook for 30 minutes.

      Add mushrooms, stir, and cook uncovered 10 minutes longer or until water is absorbed.

Yield: 20 servings.

BALSAMIC ROASTED PORK WITH PRUNES

    One 7-pound trimmed boneless pork loin
3 cups sliced onions
6 garlic cloves, peeled and minced
2 tablespoons prepared herbes de Provence
1 teaspoon freshly ground black pepper
½ teaspoon ground allspice
½ cup balsamic vinegar
¼ cup olive oil
1 pound pitted prunes
1 cup burgundy or comparable wine

In refrigerator, marinate pork loin in all ingredients except prunes and wine for 2 to 6 hours, turning occasionally.

    Preheat oven to 375°F.

    Place pork and marinade in a shallow uncovered roaster and baste.

    Roast for 30 minutes. Lower oven temperature to 325°F. Roast 45 minutes longer. Add prunes and wine and roast for about 1 hour longer or until internal temperature registers 160°F on a meat thermometer. Remove pork and prunes to warm platter.

    Reduce sauce and adjust flavor. Slice pork before serving and plate with prunes and sauce.

Yield: 20 servings.

Vegetables

PUMPKIN-GINGER MOUSSE

⅓ cup brandy
2 teaspoons unflavored gelatin
½ cup chopped candied ginger
4 eggs, separated
1 teaspoon cream of tartar
⅔ cup sugar
4 cups pumpkin puree
  1 (29 ounce) can solid-pack pumpkin can be substituted
1 teaspoon ground cinnamon
½ teaspoon ground ginger
¼ teaspoon ground cloves
  juice and grated zest of 1 orange
1 pint vanilla ice cream
1 cup heavy cream, whipped
½ cup chopped, toasted almonds

Oil a 6-inch-wide strip of parchment paper and tie a collar around a 3-quart soufflé dish so that paper stands up 2 inches from the rim.

Warm brandy in a small saucepan. Remove from heat and stir in gelatin until dissolved. Add chopped ginger. Set aside.

In a small bowl, beat the egg whites and cream of tartar with electric mixer at high speed. Set aside.

In a large bowl, beat egg yolks and sugar with electric mixer for 3 minutes. Stir in pumpkin, cinnamon, ginger, cloves, orange juice, and zest. Add gelatin mixture. Stir in softened ice cream until well blended.

Alternately add whipped cream and beaten egg whites. Spoon into soufflé dish and cover with chopped almonds. Freeze for 30 minutes or refrigerate 6 hours or until chilled.

Yield: 20 servings.

CRANBERRY-BEET COMPOTE

- 2 pounds cranberries
- ⅔ cup sugar
- ⅔ cup water
- 2 pounds beets, cooked and diced
- 1 cup red currant jelly
- ½ cup Campari (optional)

In a heavy saucepan, combine cranberries, sugar, and water. Bring to a boil. Reduce heat when the berries start to pop. Add beets, and stir for about 10 minutes. Add red currant jelly, stirring until dissolved.

Place in serving dish and refrigerate, covered, until ready to serve.

Yield: 20 servings.

MAPLE GLAZED APPLES, PEARS, AND ONIONS

- 5 Granny Smith apples
- 5 Bosc pears
- 2 Spanish onions
- 3 red onions
- 2 tablespoons unsalted butter
- 2 tablespoons safflower oil
- 1 cup maple syrup

Core apples and pears. Slice vertically, but do not peel. Peel and slice onions.

In a large heavy skillet, heat butter and oil. Sauté onions for about 12 minutes over moderate heat. Add apple and pear slices and sauté for another 5 minutes. Lower heat and stir in maple syrup. Serve hot.

Yield: 20 servings.

SAUTÉED BRUSSELS SPROUTS AND CHESTNUTS

     2 quarts Brussels sprouts
     2 tablespoons unsalted butter
     2 tablespoons safflower oil
    12 ounces freshly peeled, cooked chestnuts
        salt and freshly ground pepper to taste

Trim Brussels sprouts. Bring a large pot of water to a boil and boil Brussels sprouts for 5 minutes. Drain.

Heat butter and oil in large heavy skillet over low to moderate heat. Add Brussels sprouts and cook for 15 minutes, stirring occasionally. Add chestnuts and sauté another 10 minutes. Season with salt and pepper. Serve hot.

Yield: 20 servings.

ROASTED ROOT VEGETABLES

     4 pounds white potatoes
     4 pounds carrots, scraped
     4 pounds parsnips, scraped
     1 large head celery
     3 heads garlic
    ½ cup olive oil
        sweet paprika
    ½ cup minced parsley leaves

Preheat oven 400°F. Bring water to boil in a medium
pot.

Peel potatoes, carrots, and parsnips. Separate celery
stalks and destring them. Cut all into 3 × ¾-inch pieces
and boil gently for 5 minutes and drain.

Separate and peel garlic cloves. Oil lasagna or sheet
pan and spread vegetables and garlic cloves over. Drizzle
with remaining oil. Sprinkle with paprika. Roast for 45
minutes. Arrange vegetables on platter and top with
minced parsley.

Yield: 20 servings.

EGGPLANTS AND APRICOTS

12 thin Chinese eggplants
½ pound dried apricots, diced
¼ cup safflower oil
2 tablespoons minced peeled gingerroot
6 shallots, minced
2 tablespoons Chinese chili paste
½ cup low-sodium soy sauce
1 teaspoon sugar dissolved in 1 tablespoon vinegar
1 cup water or chicken broth
1 tablespoon sesame oil

Discard base and tip of eggplants. Cut eggplants into
lengthwise quarters and then across into 1½-inch chunks.
Pour boiling water over apricots. Let stand for 15
minutes and drain.

In a wok or skillet, heat oil and add ginger and
eggplant, stirring until lightly browned. Add scallions and
apricots and stir for a few minutes more.

Mix remaining ingredients and pour into pan. Cook

for about 10 minutes, until eggplant is tender but still firm.

Yield: 20 servings.

STIR-FRIED SNOW PEAS, CARROTS, AND WATER CHESTNUTS

  3 pounds snow peas
  5 carrots
  1 pound water chestnuts

Trim ends and strings, if any, from peas. Scrape carrots and cut into julienne. Scrub, peel, and slice water chestnuts just before cooking.

Yield: 20 servings.

SPINACH WITH SHALLOTS, PINE NUTS, AND RAISINS

  6 pounds fresh spinach
  ¾ cup minced peeled shallots
  ⅓ cup pine nuts
  ⅓ cup raisins
  6 tablespoons unsalted butter
     juice and zest of 1 lemon
     freshly grated nutmeg
     coarse (kosher) salt and freshly ground pepper to taste

Trim spinach, rinse, and drain, but do not dry. In large skillet, sauté shallots, pine nuts, and raisins in butter.

Add spinach with the water still clinging to the leaves and stir in pound by pound as it wilts. Cook 10 minutes or until cooked through.

Remove from heat add lemon juice and zest. Season to taste with nutmeg, salt, and pepper. Serve hot.

Yield: 20 servings.

ASPARAGUS DRIZZLED WITH CREAM

  5 pounds asparagus
  3 cups heavy cream
  3 1-inch pieces gingerroot, peeled
     grated zest of 2 lemons

Break off tough ends of asparagus and trim only if necessary. Bring salted water to a boil and simmer asparagus 5 minutes or until firm-tender. Set on warm platter.

In small heavy saucepan, heat cream over moderate heat. Press ginger and extract liquid into cream. Drop ginger pieces in cream along with lemon zest. Keep stirring until cream is reduced to about 2½ cups. Remove ginger and pour over asparagus (about 2 tablespoons per portion).

Yield: 20 servings.

STIR-FRIED BROCCOLI

 12 medium broccoli stalks
  ¼ cup safflower oil
  ½ cup sesame oil
  2 bunches watercress
  ½ cup low-sodium soy sauce or oyster sauce
 12 garlic cloves, peeled and crushed
  ¼ cup toasted sesame seeds

Separate broccoli florets and slice stems on diagonal. Bring water to a boil and parboil broccoli for 4 minutes. Drain.

In wok or large skillet, heat oils and garlic. Stir in broccoli and watercress. Cook, stirring, 6 minutes or until crisp-tender. Stir in toasted sesame seeds. Serve hot or cold.

Yield: 20 servings.

ZUCCHINI IN LEMON-MINT BUTTER

12 young (not mini) yellow zucchini
20 young green zucchini
¾ cup (1½ sticks) unsalted butter
    skinned red pepper, seeded and diced
    skinned yellow pepper, seeded and diced
⅔ cup minced mint leaves
    juice of 3 lemons

Scrub zucchini and trim stem and flower ends. Cut in half crosswise and lengthwise. Boil zucchini for 8 to 10 minutes until crisp-tender. In a skillet, melt butter and stir in diced peppers and mint leaves. When pepper is wilted, not browned, remove from heat and stir in lemon juice. Stir into zucchini.

Yield: 20 servings.

Desserts and Sweets

Professional bakers and students use the "bakers percent" system, which is recommended by the American Institute of Baking. The Institute is a good resource for both educational advice and information. Membership allows you hotline information calls to answer specific questions. Eventually foodservice professionals need to bake and scale up by using weight measures.

For the most part, beginning caterers, who do not yet have professional ovens and equipment, usually cannot do really large-scale baking. The 18 × 26-inch sheet pan or the many layers needed for volume presentation will not be accommodated by domestic ovens. They can, however, use a 13 × 18-inch half sheet, which will serve 24 and can be made in multiples.

The following cakes and tidbits can be made in a variety of ovens including portable convection ovens. Though many start-up caterers use the services of professional bakers, even a simple cake baked from the best ingredients, and decorated with candied flowers mixed with edible ones and tied with a foil mesh ribbon, or plated with fresh berries and a dollop of whipped cream, will satisfy your guests and please your accountant.

These cakes can be mixed and matched for attractive buffet service. Several of them freeze well and many unused portions can be used for trifles and toast slices for tea. They are not fancy and are quite forgiving. If there is any difficulty in transporting even a small cake, the final assembly and trimming can be done on location.

ALMOND BISCOTTI

 1 pound slivered almond
 ½ cup granulated sugar
 2 cups all-purpose flour
 1½ cups packed light-brown sugar
 1½ teaspoons ground cinnamon
 1 teaspoon baking powder
 ¼ cup (½ stick) unsalted butter
 3 eggs, slightly beaten

Preheat oven to 350°F. Lightly grease and flour a baking sheet.

Toast almonds in a single layer on a baking sheet for 10 minutes. Leave oven on and remove almonds. Cool. Place 1 cup of almonds and granulated sugar in processor and pulse until almonds are the consistency of medium-fine bread crumbs.

In a large mixing bowl, stir flour, cinnamon, baking powder, and almond mixture. Put remaining almonds in processor with butter and process 3 or 4 seconds until chunky. Add to flour mixture and blend in eggs. Knead until all ingredients are incorporated.

Divide dough in half and form into ropes about 1 inch in diameter and place side by side on prepared baking sheet. Flatten gently.

Bake for 20 minutes or until lightly browned.

Remove from oven and if dough is at all raw, place back in oven for 5 minutes. Cut rolls into ¾-inch slices, leaving them on the baking sheets. Turn oven off and let slices stand in oven for 20 minutes. Cool on wire racks. Store in airtight container.

Yield: 40.

CURLED ALMOND TILES

   2 egg whites
   1 egg yolk
   ½ cup sugar
   ½ teaspoon vanilla extract
   3 tablespoons unsalted butter, melted and cooled
   3 tablespoons all-purpose flour
   2 tablespoons ground almonds
   ½ cup sliced almonds

Preheat oven to 400°F. Grease and lightly flour baking sheets.

In medium bowl, beat egg whites, sugar, and vanilla with electric mixer for 3 minutes or until the mixture is syrupy. Incorporate butter, flour, and ground almonds.

Drop by teaspoons onto prepared pans and spread gently into 2-inch circles. Sprinkle with almond slices. Leave 3 inches between cookies. Make 12 at a time unless you have an assistant to speed the curling process.

Bake 4 minutes and immediately lift warm cookies one by one with a spatula and curl over a cannoli mold or a rolling pin.

Flat cookies can be returned to warm oven to soften if they harden while you are preparing the curls. When they are completely cool and crisp they can be stored in a tightly closed tin.

Yield: 36.

ANGEL FOOD CAKE

    whites from 12 eggs
2 teaspoons cream of tartar
1 tablespoons lemon juice
1¼ cups granulated sugar
1½ teaspoons vanilla extract
1½ cups cake flour
2¾ cups confectioners' sugar

Preheat oven to 350°F. Set out ungreased 10-inch angel food tube pan. Beat egg whites with electric mixture and, as they start to stiffen, slowly add cream of tartar and lemon juice. As they stiffen more, gradually add granulated sugar and vanilla until soft peaks form.

In a separate bowl, mix flour and confectioners' sugar. Gently fold into egg whites.

Turn into tube pan and bake for 30 minutes or until

cake springs back when lightly touched. Cool in inverted pan. If pan does not have "legs," invert over funnel or bottle.

Yield: One 10-inch tube cake.

BERRY SUMMER PUDDING

 1 pound strawberries
 1 pound blueberries
 1 pound raspberries
 1 pound blackberries or pitted cherries
 2 cups sugar
 1 large loaf of standard white bread
 4 ounces sweet whipped butter
   frozen yogurt or crème fraîche

Place all berries in a bowl of water to drain of any grit. Place in colander until dry. Hull and return to bowl and stir with sugar.

Trim crusts from bread and butter them. Line pudding bowl or charlotte mold with bread slices, butter-side out. Place one third of berries in mold, and with buttered bread slices, press berries up the sides. Put another one third of berries in bowl and repeat, filling with remaining berries and topping with sliced bread, butter-side down.

Place a plate or removable tart tin bottom on top to press mixture down. Put a weight on top and refrigerate for several hours, up to a day. Unmold and serve with a scoop of frozen yogurt or a dollop of crème fraîche.

Yield: 20 servings.

BOURBON-PECAN BREAD PUDDING

  2 cups pecan halves
12 jumbo eggs
1½ cups sugar
1½ quarts skim milk
  1 cup bourbon
  1 tablespoon vanilla extract
  3 large loaves Italian bread, cut into 80 slices
  2 cups plumped raisins
 ¼ cup (½ stick) butter, softened for pan
  1 teaspoon freshly grated nutmeg
     heavy cream for garnish

Preheat oven to 350°F. Butter a 12 × 20-inch, deep sheet pan.

Spread pecans in a single layer on baking sheet and toast for 5 minutes. Set aside.

In bowl large enough to hold all ingredients, beat eggs and 1¼ cups of the sugar with electric mixer until thick. Stir in milk, bourbon, and vanilla. Soak bread in egg mixture until center is soggy. Fold raisins and reserved nuts into bread batter.

Place bread, layer by layer, on prepared pan. Pour remaining batter over all. (May be refrigerated up to 3 hours before baking.)

Place pudding pan in larger pan and pour in hot water to depth of 1 inch.

Bake 30 to 45 minutes or until knife inserted in center comes out clean.

Top with nutmeg before serving. Accompany with cream whipped with maple sugar.

Yield: 20 servings.

WILD-RICE CARROT CAKE

    6 eggs, separated
    1 cup granulated sugar
    2 cups packed brown sugar
    2 cups safflower oil
    3 cups grated carrots
    3 cups skim milk
    1 tablespoon vanilla extract
    4 cups all-purpose flour
    1 tablespoon baking powder
    2 teaspoons baking soda
    1 tablespoon ground cinnamon
    1 tablespoon ground nutmeg
    4 cups cooked wild rice
    1 cup flaked coconut
    1 can (8 ounces) crushed pineapple in pineapple juice,
      drained

    Cream Cheese Topping:
    20 ounces light cream cheese, at room temperature
    1½ pounds confectioners' sugar
       sour cream to make it spreadable

Preheat to 375°F. Lightly grease and flour a 13 × 18 × 3-inch pan.

Beat eggs and sugars together in a bowl large enough to hold all ingredients. Add oil and carrots. Stir in milk and vanilla.

Mix flour, baking powder, baking soda, cinnamon, and nutmeg together. In separate bowl, combine wild rice, coconut, and pineapple. Alternately add flour and rice mixtures to liquid in bowl. Pour into prepared pan.

Bake 50 minutes to 1 hour or until tester comes out clean. Mix Cream Cheese Topping ingredients and spread

on cooled cake or individual portions. Miniature
marzipan carrots are an attractive decoration.

Yield: 24 servings.

CHOCOLATE TERRINE
IN WHITE-CHOCOLATE BLIZZARD

¼ cup (½ stick) butter, melted
½ cup brewed espresso
2 tablespoons coffee liqueur
½ teaspoon ground cinnamon
2 cups sugar
1 cup (2 sticks) unsalted butter
2 ounces unsweetened chocolate
6 ounces bittersweet chocolate
5 eggs

White-Chocolate Blizzard Frosting:
¾ cup heavy cream
6 ounces white chocolate
¼ cup (½ stick) unsalted butter
2 tablespoons framboise or other berry *eau de vie*

Preheat oven to 325°F. Line a buttered 9 × 5 × 3-inch
loaf pan with aluminum foil and brush thoroughly with
melted butter.

In a small saucepan, heat coffee, coffee liqueur,
cinnamon, and 1 tablespoon of sugar. Stir until sugar is
dissolved. Remove from heat.

Cut butter and chocolate into chunks and melt
together in saucepan over low heat.

In a large bowl, beat eggs and remaining sugar with
an electric mixer for 5 minutes or until mixture forms a

ribbon when dropped from a beater. Stir in cooled coffee mixture, then chocolate mixture.

Pour into prepared pan. Cover securely and set into large pan with hot water not reaching the top of loaf pan.

Bake 1½ hours or until firm. Chill thoroughly on wire rack before turning out and frosting.

For frosting, heat and stir cream in a heavy saucepan, until surface starts to roll. Lower heat and, without letting it boil, stir to thicken.

Chop chocolate and butter into small bits. Add to thickened cream. Keep stirring until mixture is smooth. Turn into bowl add framboise and stir until lukewarm.

Spread on whole terrine. Scrape with decorating comb to form swirls and ridges. If desired, decorate with meringue mushrooms and/or candied roses and violets. Refrigerate until ready to serve. May be frozen after frosting. Serve at room temperature.

Yield: 20 servings.

CHOCOLATE AND CHOCOLATE CAKE

½ cup (1 stick) unsalted butter, at room temperature
2½ cups packed light-brown sugar
1 cup sour cream
3 large eggs
1 tablespoon vanilla extract
4 ounces unsweetened chocolate, melted
2 cups all-purpose flour
2 teaspoons baking powder
1 teaspoon baking soda
½ teaspoon salt
2 cups chocolate chips
Chocolate Cream (recipe, page 231)

Preheat oven to 350°F. Grease and lightly flour a 10-inch tube pan with removable bottom.

Cream butter with electric mixer until fluffy. Beat in sugar, then sour cream, eggs, vanilla, and melted chocolate.

Stir together flour, baking powder, baking soda, and salt and stir into chocolate batter. Mix until well blended. Fold in chocolate chips. Pour batter into prepared pan. Bake 45 to 55 minutes or until tester comes out clean. Cool on wire rack for 30 minutes, then remove from pan. Serve with Chocolate Cream.

Yield: One 10-inch tube cake.

CHOCOLATE CREAM

6 ounces sweet chocolate
2 cups heavy cream, whipped
2 teaspoons vanilla extract

Melt chocolate in small saucepan, adding up to ¼ cup water to make a smooth syrup. Whip cream with vanilla. Blend cream and chocolate together. Serve with seasonal berries.

Yield: 4 cups.

MADELEINES

2 eggs
1 cup sugar
1 cup all-purpose flour
¾ cup (1½ sticks) unsalted butter, melted and cooled
grated zest of 1 lemon
confectioners' sugar

Preheat oven to 350°F. Grease and lightly flour madeleine pans.

In top of double boiler over hot, not boiling, water, beat eggs and sugar for 2 minutes or until warm and blended.

Place top of double boiler in bowl of ice water and continue beating for 5 minutes.

Remove from ice water and alternately blend in flour and cooled melted butter and lemon zest. Stir only until blended.

Use one tablespoon of batter for each madeleine or follow pan manufacturer's directions.

Bake for 12 minutes. Cool 1 minute in pan. Remove from pan and cool on wire racks. Sprinkle with confectioners' sugar.

Yield: 40.

PASTEL PETITS FOURS

  7 eggs, separated
  2 teaspoons lemon juice
  9 tablespoons sugar
  ½ teaspoon vanilla extract
  ½ teaspoon almond extract
  ½ cup cold water
  ¾ teaspoon cream of tartar
1½ cups cake flour
  ¼ teaspoon salt

Icing:
white from 1 egg
  2 cups *sifted* confectioners' sugar
up to ½ cup water
candied violets, roses, and silver dragees for decoration

Preheat oven at 350°F. In a large bowl, beat egg yolks for 5 minutes. Set aside.

In medium bowl, combine lemon juice, sugar, vanilla, almond extract, and cold water and mix until sugar is dissolved. Beat egg whites with cream of tartar until opaque peaks are formed. Combine flour and salt. Mix lemon mixture into beaten egg yolks, then fold in egg whites. Gently fold in flour mixture.

Bake in two ungreased 9-inch square cake pans for 30 minutes or until cakes spring back when touched. Cool on wire racks and cut each into 12 diamonds, squares, and triangles ready to be iced.

For icing, stir egg white into sugar and gradually add water to make spreadable paste. Quickly divide into 4 small containers and tint lightly with food coloring. Frost petit fours. Decorate with candied violets, roses, and silver dragees.

Yield: 24.

MOCHA CREAM CAKE

Vanilla Sponge Layers:
  6 eggs
1⅓ cups sugar
  2 teaspoons vanilla extract
1½ cups all-purpose flour
  3 tablespoons cornstarch
  ¼ cup (½ stick) butter melted butter
     Mocha Buttercream (recipe, page 234)
     chocolate curls, chocolate-covered coffee beans, or crushed toasted nuts for garnish

Preheat oven to 350°F. Butter and flour two 9-inch layer cake pans.

In small nonreactive saucepan, beat eggs, gradually incorporating sugar. Continue beating and set over low heat until egg mixture is quite warm. Remove from heat, transfer to a bowl, and continue beating until cool. Add vanilla.

Mix flour and cornstarch and add to egg mixture. Pour into prepared pans.

Bake 20 to 25 minutes or until tester comes out clean. Cool 10 minutes, then remove from pans and cool on wire rack.

Fill and frost immediately, or freeze for use within one month. Fill and top with Mocha buttercream, or fill with mocha and cover with chocolate.

Garnish with chocolate curls, chocolate-covered coffee beans, or crushed toasted nuts.

Yield: One 9-inch layer cake.

MOCHA BUTTERCREAM

    yolks from 3 eggs
½ cup sugar
½ cup brewed espresso
1 cup (2 sticks) unsalted butter, cut in small dice
2 tablespoons coffee liqueur

In a small bowl, beat egg yolks with electric mixer until light.

In small heavy saucepan, bring sugar and espresso to a boil, lower heat, and simmer 2 to 3 minutes.

Pour coffee in a thin stream into egg yolks and keep beating. Return mixture to saucepan set over very low heat and beat for 5 or 6 minutes or until mixture coats a wooden spoon.

Quickly beat in butter and coffee liqueur and remove

from heat, stirring until fluffy. Mixture will thicken as it stands.

Yield: 2 cups.

CHOCOLATE BUTTERCREAM CAKE

2 Vanilla Sponge layers (recipe, page 233)
½ cup heavy cream
½ cup (1 stick) unsalted butter
4 ounces bittersweet chocolate
2 ounces milk chocolate

Heat cream in small saucepan and stir just until surface ripples. Lower heat and stir 3 or 4 minutes. Stir in butter and chocolates mixing until mixture is shiny. Follow instructions for preceeding Mocha Cream Cake.

Yield: One 9-inch layer cake.

WALNUT EGGNOG CAKE

1½ cups (3 sticks) unsalted butter, at room temperature
2 cups sugar
6 eggs, separated
⅔ cup milk
½ cup cognac or brandy
1 teaspoon vanilla extract
2 cups unbleached flour
2 cups whole-wheat flour
1 teaspoon cream of tartar
2 cups broken walnut pieces
confectioners' sugar for garnish

Preheat oven to 275°F. Grease and lightly flour a deep 10-inch tube pan.

Cream butter and sugar with electric mixer until thoroughly combined. Beat in egg yolks. Combine milk, cognac, and vanilla. Combine the 4 cups of flour and add to butter mixture alternately with liquid.

Beat egg whites with cream of tartar until almost stiff. Add walnuts to batter, then fold in beaten egg whites. Pour into prepared pan.

Bake 2¼ hours. Cool upright for 30 minutes, invert, and cool 1 hour longer. Decorate with confectioners' sugar.

Yield: One 10-inch tube cake.

QUANTITY RECIPE DIRECTORY

Alaska Seafood Marketing Institute
    1111 West 8 Street, Suite 100
    Janeau, AK 99801-1895
    Phone: (907) 586-2902

Alaskan Harvest
    320 Seward Street
    Sitka, AK 99835
    Phone: (800) 824-6389

American Cancer Society
    Cooking Smart
    3340 Peachtree Road, N.E.
    Atlanta, GA 30026
    Phone: (800) 227-2345

American Celery Council
    Box LN
    928 Broadway
    New York, NY 10010
    Phone: (212) 420-8808 / Fax: (212) 254-2452

Can Sizes

Volume	Approximate Cups	Canners Designation	Can Number	Dimensions
4.5 ounce Fruit		208 × 203	N/A	½″ × 2³⁄₁₆″*
6 ounce Paste	⅔ cup	202 × 306	N/A	2⅛″ × 3⅜″
8 ounce Fruit (necked in)		211/208 × 305	N/A	2¹¹⁄₁₆″ / 2½″ × 3⁵⁄₁₆″
8 ounce Fruit (straight wall)	1 cup	211 × 305	#55	2¹¹⁄₁₆″ × 3⁵⁄₁₆″
11.5 ounce Tomato Juice		210 × 413	N/A	2⅝″ × 4¹³⁄₁₆″*
15 ounce Fruit/ Tomatoes	scant 2 cups	300 × 407	#300	3″ × 4⁷⁄₁₆″
¹⁶⁄₁₇ ounce Fruit/ Tomatoes	2 cups	303 × 406	#303	3³⁄₁₆″ × 4⅜″
28.5 ounces Fruit/ Tomatoes	3½ cups	401 × 411	#2½	4¹⁄₁₆″ × 4¹¹⁄₁₆″
35 ounce Tomatoes	4½ cups	404 × 502	N/A	4¼″ × 5⅛″*
46 ounce Juice/ Nectars	5¾ cups	404 × 700	#3 cylinder	4¼″ × 7″
104 ounce Fruit/ Tomatoes	12¾ cups	603 × 700	#10**	6³⁄₁₆″ × 7″

*Diameter is represented by first number and height by second; the first digit in each three digit group indicates inches and the second and third digits, sixteenths of an inch. Thus, 303 by 406 is a can 3³⁄₁₆ in diameter and 4⅜ inch in height.

**Equivalents To No. 10
    The contents of one No. 10 can equals about
        3 No. 3 cylinders
        3½ No. 2½ cans
        6 No. 303 cans

American Cheese Society
    34 Downing Street
    New York, NY 10014
    Phone: (212) 727-7939

American Heart Association
    National Center
    7320 Greenville Avenue
    Dallas, TX 75231
    Phone: (214) 373-6300

American Institute of Baking
    1213 Bakers Way
    Manhattan, KS 66502
    Phone: (800) 633-5137 / Fax: (913) 537-1493

Athens Food
    Apollo Filo Dough
    13600 Snow Road, Dept. 19
    Cleveland, OH 44142-2596
    Phone: (800) 837-5683

Ball Corporation
    345 South High Street
    Muncie, IN 47305-2326
    Phone: (317) 747-6100

Bell and Evans
    P.O. Box 39
    Fredericksburg, PA 17026
    Phone: (717) 865-6626

California Dry Bean Advisory Board
    P.O. Box 943
    Dinuba, CA 93618
    Phone: (209) 591-4866

Fleischmann's Yeast Expert
    Phone: (800) 227-6202
    (Yeast baking advice, also in French)

Florida Tomato Committee
  P.O. Box 140635
  Orlando, FL 32814-0635
  Phone: (407) 894-3071

Kansas Wheat Commission
  2630 Claflin Road
  Manhattan, KS 66502
  Phone: (913) 539-0255

Kerr Glass Manufacturing
  Consumer Affairs Department
  2444 West 16 Street
  Chicago, IL 60608
  Phone: (312) 226-1700

Louisiana Seafood Promotion & Marketing Board
  P.O. Box 70648
  New Orleans, LA 70172-0648
  Phone: (800) 222-4017

McIlhenny Co.
  Dept. 12-A
  Avery Island, LA 20513
  Phone: (800) 634-9599
  (Tabasco sauce)

Oregon Potato Commission
  700 N.E. Multnomah, Suite 460
  Portland, OR 97232
  Phone: (503) 731-3300

Superintendent of Documents
  United States Government Printing Office
  Washington, DC 20402
  Phone: (202) 783-3238
  (Ask for Bibliography 291, food and nutrition)

The Sugar Association
  1101 15 Street N.W., Suite 600
  Washington, DC 20005
  Phone: (202) 785-1122 / Fax: (202) 785-5019

United States Department of Agriculture
Human Nutrition Information Service
6505 Belcrest Road
Hyattsville, MD 20782
Phone: (301) 436-8498

Washington State Apple Commission
Tacoma, WA 98801
Phone: (509) 663-9600

FOOD RESOURCE DIRECTORY

Alaska Seafood Marketing Institute
526 Main Street
Juneau, AK 99801
Phone: (907) 586-2902
(Fish suppliers and information)

Aux Delices Des Bois
4 Leonard Street
New York, NY 10013
Phone: (212) 334-1230 / Fax: (212) 334-1231

Balducci's
(Not the retail store)
11-02 Queens Plaza South
Long Island City, NY 11101-4908
Phone: (800) 822-1444; in N.Y.: (800) 247-2450

Bazzini Company, Inc.
339 Greenwich Street
New York, NY 10013
Phone: (800) 288-0172; (212) 227-6241

Bell & Evans Chicken
P.O. Box 39
Fredericksburg, PA 17026
Phone: (717) 865-6626

Blue Gold Mussels
15 Antonia Costa Avenue
New Bedford, MA 02740
Phone: (800) 447-4443; (508) 993-2635 /
Fax: (508) 994-9508

California Dry Bean Advisory Board
P.O. Box 943
Dinuba, CA 93618
Phone: (209) 591-4866

Caprilands Herb Farm
Silver Street
Coventry, CT 06238
Phone: (203) 742-7244

Convito Italiano
11 East Chestnut
Chicago, IL 60611
Phone: (312) 943-2983

D'Artagnan, Inc.
399-419 St. Paul Avenue
Jersey City, NJ 07306
Phone: (800) DARTAGNAN / Fax: (201) 792-0588
(Foie gras, charcuterie, game)

De Choix Specialty Foods
58-25 52 Avenue
Woodside, NY 11377
Phone: (800) 332-4649; (718) 507-8080

Fines Herbes Company
16 Leonard Street
New York, NY 10013
Phone: (212) 334-9022 / Fax: (212) 334-9116

Franklin Mushroom Farms
P.O. Box 18
North Franklin, CT 06254
Phone: (203) 642-7551 / Fax: (203) 642-6407

Hotel Bar Foods
650 New Country Road
Secaucus, NJ 07094
Phone: (201) 865-3000 / Fax: (201) 865-8261
(Butter)

K-Paul's Louisiana Mail Order
824 Distributors Row
P.O. Box 23342
New Orleans, LA 70183-0342
Phone: (800) 457-2857

La Preferida, Inc.
3400 West 35 Street
Chicago, IL 60632
Phone: (312) 254-7200 / Fax: (312) 254-8546
(Foods from Mexico, South America, West Indies)

Legal Seafoods Market
237 Hampshire Street
Cambridge, MA 02139
Phone: (800) 343-5804; (617) 864-3400

Los Chileros de Nuevo Mexico
Gourmet New Mexican Foods
P.O. Box 6215
Santa Fe, NM 87502
Phone: (505) 471-6967

McIlhenny Co.
Dept. 12-A
Avery Island, LA 70513
Phone: (800) 634-9599
(Tabasco sauce)

Paprikas Weiss
1546 Second Avenue
New York, NY 10028
Phone: (212) 288-6117

Phillips Mushroom Farms
   P.O. Box 190, Kennet Square
   Kennet, PA 19348
   Phone: (800) 722-8818 / Fax: (215) 444-4751

Pike Place Fish
   86 Pike Place
   Seattle, WA 98101
   Phone: (206) 682-7181

Price Club
   Membership information and locations
   P.O. Box 85466
   San Diego, CA 92138-5466
   Phone: (619) 581-4682 / Fax: (619) 581-4793

Rena Chocolates à la Carte
   16760 Stagg Street, Suite 218
   Van Nuys, CA 91406-1642
   Phone: (800) 966-7440; (818) 786-7440 /
      Fax: (818) 786-7428

Robison State Herb Garden
   Cornell University Campus Plantation
   One Plantation Road
   Ithaca, NY 14850
   Phone: (607) 255-3020

S. Wallace Edwards & Sons
   Box 25
   Surry, VA 23883
   Phone: (800) 222-4267; (804) 294-3121

Sahadi Importing Co., Inc.
   Middle Eastern Foods
   187 Atlantic Avenue
   Brooklyn, NY 11201
   Phone: (718) 624-4550 / Fax: (718) 643-4415

Santa Fe Cooking School Market
116 West San Francisco Street
Santa Fe, NM 87501
Phone: (505) 983-4511

Sitka Sound Seafood
329-333 Katlian Street
Sitka, AK 99835
Phone: (907) 747-6867
(Catalog sales)

Uwajimaya
P.O. Box 3003
Seattle, WA 98114
Phone: (206) 624-6248

Wild Rice Company
P.O. Box 1751
Bemidji, MN 56601
Phone: (800) 243-7423

Beverages

After all the food selections have been made, the caterer has to determine what beverages are to be served. Does the client want to provide bottled water, and if so, what kind? Basic uncarbonated water, tap or bottled, should be available at all events. Supplying carbonated mineral water, mixers, and flavored sodas depends on the nature of the event and the client's preferences.

Iced tea is a very popular drink and is easy to have on hand. Urns of varying sizes for coffee, decaf, and assorted teas are usually required. Espresso machines are available for purchase and rental and are being called for more frequently, not only for demitasse but cappuccino as well.

As for alcohol, it has become increasingly the situation that events have wine and/or beer and a variety of water and fruit drinks, rather than a full bar.

Once you have a license to do business as a caterer, you may apply for a liquor license. Applications and requirements vary from state to state. Contact your state alcohol commission for information. Your lawyer will provide guidelines on your responsibilities when catering a party for which you are ordering and serving liquor. He or she will also help you decide whether you want a liquor license. A liquor license can sometimes be obtained on a time by time basis, generally for things like cash bars at fund-raisers. Your lawyer and state alcohol commission are the source for specific information.

Most distributors have information about reasonable amounts

required to stock a full bar. For wine, the Sommelier Society is most helpful in their educational information, courses, meetings, tastings, and general advice. Taking even a few classes is extremely helpful. The Educational Foundation of the National Restaurant Association offers many, and graduates will receive a responsible manager or server certificate. It is an important issue and must be considered from many viewpoints that leave the caterer hospitable and accountable. It is necessary to be generous and to control alcohol consumption.

As for selecting wines, reading is helpful, but it really is the liquid in the bottle that is the ultimate learning experience. There is a lot to know, as people are more and more interested in wine, well past red or white. A few phone calls will start you networking, and you will soon discover what the area prizewinners are.

It is good to establish a relationship with a well-stocked liquor store in your neighborhood, so that suggestions will be knowledgeable, prices good, and returns accepted for unused bottles. As usual, however, if it is not something you want to focus on, be sure you have qualified bar help you can hire and with whom you can consult.

Often the client will order the liquor directly to their taste or on your recommendation of selections and quantity. If there are no specific requests, the needs of contemporary diners are usually met with good quality Bordeaux and Chardonnay—the Chardonnay served well chilled, and the red *a chambre* or about 60°F. Good quality is the secret—it is the difference between a satisfying experience and a passable one. As with food, the best quality comfortably affordable is chosen because the taste has more resonance, so it actually takes a smaller measure to satisfy the palate.

A Beaujolais Nouveau has the advantage of tasting better on the cool side and can be served from its presentation in the fall until May 1. In the summer chilled Tavel is an extremely pleasant rosé and there are several Italian frizzante wines with a light tingle that are refreshing. International selections in all classes will suit the occasion and the people you are catering to. From the various regions of Italy and Spain to Australia and Chile come flavorful and discrete wines. Like the food, it should please without being overwhelming or breaking the bank. There are also more and more viticultural designations in this country that are producing excellent wines that deserve acknowledgment. Regional wines you grow to know will become good choices, though they can be a little expensive.

Fortified wines, like sherry, port, or Vino Santo are usually served when there is a full bar or, of course, if they are specifically requested for dessert. Brandies, cognacs, liqueurs, and *eaux de vie* occasionally accompany coffee and tea. For special service you can rent a liqueur cart from which to serve them at each table.

When wines and liquors are stocked for cooking, the appropriate portions are factored into the cost of the dish, not with the beverages. Sweet and savory sauces, marinades, and deglazing are often enhanced with specially chosen aromatic spirits. Crepes, cakes, and mousses are often made with liqueurs. In most states no license is needed for this use.

More often champagne or méthode champenoise wines are offered for their versatility and the celebratory mood they set. They are equally good with hors d'oeuvres, desserts, or after-dinner dancing. Jeroboams, which contain the equivalent of four bottles, are sometimes used for champagne toasts. The giant-sized Nebuchadnezzar, which holds the equivalent of eighteen bottles, is used on rare showy events.

The very best champagne is best drunk pure and in small amounts for small groups. Often moderately priced ones are delicious, and discovering them is a challenge to the skill and taste of the purchaser. There are classic champagne drinks like champagne cocktails, mimosas, and bellinis that are served not only for brunches but for summer parties as well. Fresh peach or orange juice and bitters can be kept at the bar. The addition of framboise or crème de cassis creates the popular Kir Royale.

Unless your client has no preference, don't order a case or more of wine that you yourself have not tasted and approved, preferably with a second opinion. Your wine purveyor will be helpful, as will your network of friends and acquaintances. Don't be shy about asking until you build up a repertoire of wines for various meals and events. It makes sense to go to some wine tastings before catering them. A caterer does not have to build a wine cellar as many restaurants do. As a result, there is an opportunity to grow into a connoisseur. There is nothing wrong in repeatedly serving labels and vintages you know and trust as you expand your palate.

A "kir" is usually white wine and creme de cassis, served over ice or not. Made with red wine, it is called a Cardinale. Framboise is another good champagne or white wine mixer. Spritzers are a way to serve something festive with reduced alcohol and calories. Punches are again coming into favor as people are becoming more adventurous and contemporary versions are treated with style and a light hand. They are served warm and mulled in the winter and icy cold in the summer, with citrus fruit and spices or aromatic herbs.

Another item to check is whether the premises such as a public park forbid or require a special license or permit for liquor to be served on a single-function basis. The obligations of the caterer, the host, and the bar server must be defined.

No minor is to be served alcohol, no intoxicated person can be served, and pregnant women must be notified of the potential dangers of alcohol. Any guest who is deemed under the influence must not be permitted to drive from the event. It is necessary to talk with your lawyer about who is responsible for what.

Logic dictates the host must be discreetly informed that a guest needs transportation home. The staff never drinks.

Most wine is bottled in 75 centiliter bottles which equals twenty-four ounces. A standard bottle will provide six four-ounce glasses each; sparkling wines and champagne pours seven glasses a bottle. With meals the following are average portions; lunch 1.5 glasses a person; an evening party, two glasses; and for a full dinner, two to three glasses each.

If there are two kinds of wine, it might come out to two glasses of each per wine per guest. For a lengthy affair you may want an extra case of whatever is being served.

If the client requests it, good-label bottles of bourbon, gin, scotch, and vodka are easily stocked along with tonic, seltzer, cranberry, grapefruit, orange, and tomato juices. Lemon and lime sections and Worcestershire and Tabasco sauces can be on hand at the bar also.

Sometimes a specific pitcher of cocktails is requested. Whether it is margaritas, sangria, daiquiris, piña coladas, martinis, or Bloody Marys, follow your favorite recipe, or that of your client, setting the portion of alcohol at about two ounces a drink.

There is some equipment like good quality corkscrews, bottle and can openers, paring knives, and zesters that you want to own. Skewers, stirrers, straws, swizzle sticks, small doilies, and cocktail napkins can be bought inexpensively in bulk. Bar shakers and strainers, buckets and stands can be rented. Containers for ice will vary with the service style. It may be useful to have a few conventional-size ones for small bar setups and large ones for locations that do not have ice makers or adequate freezer storage.

Consider buying a supply of stemmed red and white wine glasses as well as water and iced tea glasses. You will use them enough to warrant the purchase. If the client wants something special, they can be rented.

Always have water available for guests when you serve wine or any alcohol so that they do not quench their thirst with liquor. Wine is only a more moderate drink than hard liquor because it is generally sipped and accompanied by food, either hors d'oeuvres, dinner, or dessert.

COFFEE

Good coffee always brings smiles and no one forgives a bad cup. People are very passionate about the flavor. Aromatic or artificially flavored coffees would seem to have no place on a food menu. Use the best and freshest grade of a standard house blend for standard cups of coffee and decaf. The increasingly popular espresso is a simple addition and cappuccino only a little more labor intensive.

For standard coffee the measure is one coffee measure (two level tablespoons) to three-quarter cup water. Keep everything very clean as oil residue builds up and breeds germs and attracts dirt. For this reason it is not a good idea to use a brewer of over twenty-five servings. Only 80 percent of your guests will want coffee these days and one third of them will probably want decaf.

There are so many coffees from all over the world and so many ways of roasting, grinding, and preparing them, that the chemical addition of other flavors overpowers the bouquet of a really good cup of coffee or espresso. The artificial aromatic blends have a bit too much perfume and are not the best complement for a meal.

Jan Anderson at Illycafe was very clear about the importance of organization in coffee service. Illycafe in New York and elsewhere will rent espresso/cappuccino machines and either train someone to use it or supply a server. During its use someone must be responsible for the machine.

Large machines require 220 volts, but for the most part they do not have to be hooked up to a water supply. One or more five-gallon jugs of water are set under a skirted table or cart and a self-contained pump in the machine pulls the water up through a tube set in the neck of the jug. The espresso/cappuccino station should be set up, with the demitasse cups warming on top of the machine and milk for cappuccino kept cold in thermos jugs. In warm weather, skim milk will make perfect foam. Illycafe espresso, both regular and decaf, can be supplied in pods so that measuring is eliminated.

Coffee is becoming more and more enjoyable and interesting to people. And more than a passing nod should be given to selecting and serving it. It has become an easy way to extend social time for people looking for low-calorie and nonalcoholic pleasures.

TEA

One pound of tea equals two hundred teaspoons or two hundred tea bags, which will make two hundred cups of tea. It follows that a half pound of tea will make one hundred five-to six-ounce cups of hot tea—certainly the beverage bargain of even a party using the very best quality.

Most caterers serve tea by placing a quality tea bag on a saucer beside a cup, or in a small teapot of hot water brought to the table. For buffet serving, an assortment of tea bags—regular, decaf, and herbal—are placed on each table or at the coffee and tea station, next to an urn of near-boiling water. For a large crowd this seems the best system especially favoring herbals.

A more elegant way to serve a single kind of tea is to make it from concentrate, by pouring one quart of boiling water over two-thirds cup of tea, cover and steep for five minutes, strain into a pitcher, cover, and keep at room temperature for no more than three or four hours. Add three quarts for twenty-five cups of hot tea. Serve in a large teapot on a tray set with a pot of hot water and the option of lemon slices, milk, or cream.

The best method for hot tea is to pour freshly boiling water over the leaves and steep from three to five minutes. Clearly this is only possible for small groups.

Iced tea is a very popular beverage and an easy one to supply. For fresh iced tea, place twelve teabags or one-third cup loose tea in a large pitcher and add four cups of water that has just been brought to a boil. Sweeten or spice to taste, steep five minutes, and add four cups cold water. Add orange slices, lemon slices, whole cloves, cinnamon sticks, or fresh ginger slices and your personal blends can be individually blended.

If you are working with limited range space a microwave oven can be used to make iced teas. For two quarts: Place twelve tea bags and three cups water in 1-quart Pyrex measuring cup, run microwave at HIGH for two minutes, remove, and let stand for three minutes. Remove tea bags, sweeten to taste if desired, then add 5 cups cold water.

Attractive service pieces are often in the client's own collection and they may want to mix them with the caterer's or rental pieces. Though beverages are an accent at a meal, people are becoming more and more aware of the quality of what they imbibe. It is the caterer's task to make certain that beverage service will not in any way diminish the aura of hospitality that clients rely on.

BEVERAGE DIRECTORY

Carillon Importers Ltd.
Recipe booklets
Glenpointe Center West
Teaneck, NJ 07666-6897
Phone: (201) 836-7085

Celestial Seasonings
Consumer Services
4600 Sleepytime Drive
Boulder, CO 80301-3292
Phone: (800) 351-8175

Coca-Cola
Consumer Affairs
Phone: (800) 995-2653

Jan Anderson Illycafe
108 East 16 Street
New York, NY 10003
Phone: (212) 477-4040

International Wine Center
231 West 29 Street
New York, NY 10001
Phone: (212) 679-4190

Metro NY Area Consolidated ABC Boards
250 Broadway
New York, NY 10007
Phone: (212) 417-2026

National Coffee Association of U.S.A., Inc.
110 Wall Street
New York, NY 10005
Phone: (212) 344-5596 / Fax: (212) 425-7059

Schweppes, Pepsi, Evian
Customer Service
Phone: (203) 968-7673

Starbucks Coffee Company
Specialty Sales Department
2203 Airport Way South
Seattle, WA 98124
Phone: (800) 344-1575

State Liquor Authority of New York
250 Broadway
New York, NY 10013
Phone: (212) 417-4002

Sommelier Society of America
P.O. Box 1770, Madison Square Station
New York, NY 10159
Phone: (212) 679-4190

Tea Association of the United States
230 Park Avenue
New York, NY 10169
Phone: (212) 986-9415

Local Listings in the Yellow Pages
State Liquor Licensing Organization
Bottled Water Distributor
Discount Wine and Liquor Vendors
Wine Distributors
Restaurant Supply Houses

THIRTEEN

Public Service Perishable Food Distribution

Food networking is one way to acknowledge the hunger that some of our neighbors live with. Surplus perishable and prepared food is often difficult to distribute and many people have reported that their offerings have been refused. In many states there are "Good Samaritan" laws that permit the unlicensed redistribution of fresh and cooked food. If you want to become an independent Food Donor it is best to check with your lawyer and community health department, but any of the groups listed below will assist you in the redistribution of perishable food.

There are food rescue organizations nationwide which handle the redistribution of unused, unserved, perishable, prepared cooked, uncooked, ready-to-eat food. Any oversupply has to be handled quickly and cautiously. These local organizations not only adhere to local food safety and sanitation regulations but are up to date in a network of needful recipients so that donated food is delivered in a timely and genuinely useful way.

It is necessary to plan ahead so that surplus catered food can be given to people who would otherwise not have access to it.

Some food banks and other programs gather some perishable food but their main resources are nonperishable foods that are packaged and prepared by manufacturers, processors, distributors, and supermarkets. The following organizations support an extensive community in a link that redistributes over two million pounds of perishable food each month. By all means add to this list any additional programs you know of. Please recognize that this list, like so many others, may have changed by the time you need to reach one of the groups. Please don't be discouraged. A few phone calls starting with the Foodchain Information Hotline (800-845-3008) will assist you in finding a neighborhood link.

City Harvest in New York (212-463-0456) uses refrigerated trucks to pick up leftovers. The Community Food Network in Kansas City (816-231-3173) will help network west of the Mississippi. Second Harvest in Chicago (312-263-2303) also has useful information.

LIST OF FOODCHAIN MEMBERS AND ASSOCIATE MEMBERS

ALABAMA

Magic City Harvest
    1720 16 Avenue, South
    Birmingham, AL 35205
    Phone: (205) 933-5806

Twelve Baskets Program
    Montgomery Area Food Bank, Inc.
    521 Trade Center Street
    Montgomery, AL 36108
    Phone: (205) 263-3784 / Fax: (205) 262-6854

ARIZONA

Waste Not, Inc.
    P.O. Box 25606
    Phoenix, AZ 85002
    Phone: (602) 941-1841

ARKANSAS

Potluck, Inc.
    8400 Asher Avenue
    Little Rock, AR 72204
    Phone: (501) 568-1147 / Fax: (501) 568-1167

CALIFORNIA

Contra Costa Food Bank
5121 Port Chicago Highway
Concord, CA 94520
Phone: (510) 676-7543 / Fax: (510) 671-7933

Daily Bread
2447 Prince Street
Berkeley, CA 94705
Phone: (510) 848-3522

The FoodBank of Southern California
1444 San Francisco Avenue
Long Beach, CA 90813
Phone: (310) 435-3577 / Fax: (310) 437-6168

Extra Helpings
L.A. Regional Foodbank
1734 East 41 Street
Los Angeles, CA 90058
Phone: (213) 234-3030, x131 / Fax: (213) 234-0943

Food Rescue..for People in Need
Food Distribution Center
426-A West Almond Street
Orange, CA 92666
Phone: (714) 771-1343 / Fax: (714) 771-2748

Food Share R.P.M.'s, Inc.
4156 North Southbank Road
Oxnard, CA 93030
Phone: (805) 647-3944 / Fax: (805) 485-4156

Love's Gift Hunger Relief Program
P.O. Box 370900
San Diego, CA 92137
Phone: (619) 581-3663

Napa Valley Food Connection
P.O. Box 108
St. Helena, CA 94574
Phone: (707) 963-5183

Generous Helping
Sacramento Area Com. Kitchen
909 12th Street, Suite 200
Sacramento, CA 95814
Contact: Ms. Linda Burkholder
Phone: (916) 447-7063 / Fax: (916) 447-7052

Second Helpings
Second Harvest Food Bank of Santa Clara/
San Mateo Countys
750 Curtner Avenue
San Jose, CA 95125
Phone: (408) 266-8866 / Fax: (408) 266-9042

COLORADO
Community Food Share
5547 Central Avenue
Boulder, CO 80303
Phone: (303) 443-0623 / Fax: (303) 449-7004

Denver's Table
Food Bank of the Rockies
10975 East 47 Avenue
Denver, CO 80239
Phone: (303) 371-9250 / Fax: (303) 371-9259

Food Resource Center
Box 1497
Avon, CO 81620
Phone: (303) 845-7147

Pikes Peak Harvest
332 West Bijou, Suite 107
Colorado Springs, CO 80905
Phone: (719) 685-4594 / Fax: Same

The Prepared Food Program
The FDC of Larimer County
1301 Blue Spruce
Ft. Collins, CO 80524
Phone: (303) 493-4477 / Fax: (303) 493-5122

CONNECTICUT

Fair Share Table
   99 Old Academy Road
   Fairfield, CT 06430
   Phone: (203) 259-6463

Table To Table
   FoodBank of Lower Fairfield County
   538 Canal Street
   Stamford, CT 06902
   Phone: (203) 323-3211 / Fax: (203) 358-8306

Foodshare of Greater Hartford
   P.O. Box 2019
   Hartford, CT 06144-2019
   Phone: (203) 688-6500 / Fax: (203) 688-2776

DISTRICT OF COLUMBIA

D.C. Central Kitchen
   425 Second Street, N.W.
   Washington, DC 20001
   Phone: (202) 234-0707 / Fax: (202) 986-1051

FLORIDA

Extra Helpings of Daily Bread
   Daily Bread Food Bank
   5850 N.W. 32nd Avenue
   Miami, FL 33142
   Phone: (305) 634-5088 / Fax: (305) 633-0036

First Coast Food Runners
   Food Bank of Jacksonville
   1502 Jessie Street
   Jacksonville, FL 32206
   Phone: (904) 353-3663 / Fax: (904) 358-4281

Second Helpings
   Second Harvest FdBk. of Central Florida
   2515 Shader Road
   Orlando, FL 32804
   Phone: (407) 292-8988 / Fax: (407) 292-4758

GEORGIA

Atlanta's Table
Atlanta Community Food Bank
970 Jefferson Street N.W.
Atlanta, GA 30318
Phone: (404) 892-1250 / Fax: (404) 892-4026

Unto Others
Middle Georgia Community Food Bank
P.O. Box 5024
Macon, GA 31208
Phone: (912) 743-4580 / Fax: (912) 741-8777

Second Servings
Second Harvest of Coastal Georgia
5 Carolan Street
Savannah, GA 31401
Phone: (912) 236-6750 / Fax: (912) 238-1391

HAWAII

Hawaii's Table
Hawaii Foodbank
1320 Kalani Street, #108
Honolulu, HI 96817
Phone: (808) 847-4655 / Fax: (808) 841-5678

ILLINOIS

Prepared Foods Program
Greater Chicago Food Depository
4501 South Tripp Avenue
Chicago, IL 60632
Phone: (312) 247-3663 / Fax: (312) 247-0772

Heart of Illinois Harvest
c/o Salvation Army
P.O. Box 9702
Peoria, IL 61612
Phone: (309) 679-1379

LOUISIANA

Greater Baton Rouge Food Bank
766 Chippewa Street
Baton Rouge, LA 70805-7619
Phone: (504) 334-0288 / Fax: (504) 387-0203

MARYLAND

Food Link
80 West Street
Annapolis, MD 21401
Phone: (410) 974-8599 / Fax: (410) 974-8566

Second Helping
The Maryland Food Bank, Inc.
241 N. Franklintown Road
Baltimore, MD 21223
Phone: (410) 947-4442 / Fax: (410) 947-1853

MASSACHUSETTS

Second Helping
Greater Boston Food Bank
99 Atkinson Street
Boston, MA 02118
Phone: (617) 427-5200 / Fax: (617) 427-0146

Western Massachusetts Food Bank
P.O. Box 160
Hatfield, MA 01038
Phone: (413) 247-9738 / Fax: (413) 247-9577

M/A-COM Food Share
100 Chelmsford Street
Lowell, MA 01851
Phone: (508) 453-3100, x997 / Fax: (508) 453-0879

Food Drive For The Hungry
American Red Cross of Massachusetts/
Project Bread
61 Medford Street
Somerville, MA 02143
Phone: (617) 623-0033 / Fax: (617) 623-0355

Rachel's Table
    633 Salisburg Street
    Worcester, MA 01609
    Phone (508) 799-7699

MICHIGAN

Food Gatherers
    420 Detroit Street
    Ann Arbor, MI 48104
    Phone: (313) 761-2796 / Fax: (313) 769-1235

Forgotton Harvest
    24001 Southfield Road #205
    Southfield, MI 48075
    Phone: (313) 557-4483

MINNESOTA

Twelve Baskets
    2nd Harvest St. Paul Food Bank
    1140 Gervais Avenue
    St. Paul, MN 55117
    Phone: (612) 484-5117 / Fax: (612) 484-7431

MISSISSIPPI

The Gleaners, Inc.
    P.O. Box 9883
    Jackson, MS 39286-0883
    Phone: (601) 981-4240

MISSOURI

Kansas City Harvest
    Harvesters-The Com. Fd. Netwk.
    1811 North Topping
    Kansas City, MO 64120
    Phone: (816) 231-3173 / Fax: (816) 231-7044

Operation Food Search, Inc.
    9657 Dielman Rock Island Drive
    St. Louis, MO 63132
    Contact: Mr. William E. Nordmann
    Phone: (314) 569-0053 / Fax: (314) 569-0381

Ozarks Share-A-Meal
 Ozarks Food Harvest
 615 North Glenstone
 Springfield, MO 65802
 Phone: (417) 865-3411 / Fax: (417) 865-0504

NEBRASKA

Food Bank of Lincoln, Inc.
 4800 North 57 Street
 Lincoln, NE 68507
 Phone: (402) 466-8170 / Fax: (402) 466-6124

NEW JERSEY

Extra Helping
 Community Food Bank of N.J.
 31 Evans Terminal Road
 Hillside, NJ 07205
 Phone: (908) 355-4991 / Fax: (908) 355-0270

NEW MEXICO

The Food Brigade of Santa Fe
 121 Don Gaspar
 Santa Fe, NM 87501
 Phone: (505) 986-8288 / Fax: (505) 988-4645

NEW YORK

City Harvest
 159 West 25 Street, 10th Floor
 New York, NY 10001-7201
 Phone: (212) 463-0456 / Fax: (212) 727-2439

Food Shuttle of Western NY, Inc.
 250 St. Gregory Court
 Williamsville, NY 14221
 Phone: (716) 688-2527

Foodlink
 P.O. Box 11290
 Rochester, NY 14611
 Phone: (716) 235-5152 / Fax: (716) 235-3432

Foodshare—People to People
261 Mountainview Avenue
Nyack, NY 10960
Phone: (914) 358-4606 / Fax: (914) 353-4780

Heart and Soul
1501 Pierce Avenue
Niagara Falls, NY 14301
Phone: (716) 285-0794

Island Harvest
199 Second Street
Mineola, NY 11501
Phone: (516) 294-8528 / Fax: (516) 294-8529

Queens Interfaith Hunger Network
87-04 88 Avenue
Woodhaven, NY 11421
Phone: (718) 847-9200

The Food Shuttle
c/o The Junior League of Albany
419 Madison Avenue
Albany, NY 12216
Phone: (518) 462-1111

The Prepared Foods Program
Food Bank of Central NY
555 Stewart Drive West
North Syracuse, NY 13212
Phone: (315) 458-1554 / Fax: (315) 458-8292

NORTH CAROLINA

Greensboro's Table
605 Martin Luther King Drive
Greensboro, NC 27406
Phone: (919) 271-5975

Inter-Faith Food Shuttle
723 West Johnson Street
Raleigh, NC 27603
Phone: (919) 829-0056

NORTH DAKOTA

Daily Bread
Great Plains Food Bank
P.O. Box 389
Fargo, ND 58107
Phone: (701) 232-2624 / Fax: (701) 232-3871

OHIO

American Red Cross Emergency Food Bank
370 West First Street
Dayton, OH 45402
Phone: (513) 461-0265 / Fax: (513) 461-3316

Northcoast Harvest
2639 Wooster Road
Cleveland, OH 44116
Phone: (216) 356-9449 / Fax: (216) 356-9424

Operation FoodShare PPFP
FreeStore/FoodBank
112 East Liberty Street
Cincinnati, OH 45210
Phone: (513) 768-6452 / Fax: (513) 381-3915

Second Servings
Mid-Ohio FoodBank
1625 West Mound Street
Columbus, OH 43223
Phone: (614) 274-7770 / Fax: (614) 274-8063

OKLAHOMA

Second Helpings
Oklahoma City Food Bank
P.O. Box 26306
Oklahoma City, OK 73126
Phone: (405) 236-0543 / Fax: (405) 236-8342

Table to Table
Tulsa Community Food Bank
1150 North Iroquois Avenue
Tulsa, OK 74106
Phone: (918) 585-2800 / Fax: (918) 585-2862

OREGON

Food Rescue Express
FOOD for Lane County
255 Madison Street
Eugene, OR 97402
Phone: (503) 343-2822 / Fax: (503) 343-5019

Food Train/Food Depot
The Society of St. Vincent de Paul
3601 S.E. 27th
Portland, OR 97202
Phone: (503) 234-1114 / Fax: (503) 233-5581

The Gleaning Network
211 North Front Street
Central Point, OR 97502
Phone: (503) 664-5244

PENNSYLVANIA

Channels
259 Westover Drive
New Cumberland, PA 17070
Phone: (717) 774-8220

Three Rivers Table
Greater Pittsburgh Community FoodBank
P.O. Box 127
McKeesport, PA 15134
Phone: (412) 672-4949 / Fax: (412) 672-4740

Philabundance
4320 Main Street
Philadelphia, PA 19127
Phone: (215) 483-6444 / Fax: (215) 483-6401

South Central Pennsylvania Food Bank
P.O. Box 7409
Steelton, PA 17113
Phone: (717) 939-1611 / Fax: (717) 939-1630

RHODE ISLAND
Rhode Island Community Food Bank
P.O. Box 1325
West Warwick, RI 02893
Phone (401) 826-3072 / Fax: (401) 826-2420

SOUTH CAROLINA
Loaves & Fishes
1200 Woodruff Road, Suite A3
Greenville, SC 29607
Phone: (803) 627-9908 / Fax: (803) 288-7937

Second Helpings, Inc.
17 Hollyberry Lane
Hilton Head Island, SC 29928
Phone: (803) 671-1661

The Soup Kitchen
Charleston InterFaith Crisis Ministry
P.O. Box 20038
Charleston, SC 29413-0038
Phone: (803) 723-1476 / Fax: (803) 577-6667

TENNESSEE
Knoxville Harvest
SHARE: S. Appalachian FoodBk.
10600 Dutchtown Road
Knoxville, TN 37932
Phone: (615) 671-1211 / Fax: (615) 675-4073

Nashville's Table, Inc.
102 Woodmont Boulevard, Suite 500
Nashville, TN 37205
Phone: (615) 385-3444 / Fax: (615) 292-3305

Round Up
Memphis Food Bank
239 South Dudley Street
Memphis, TN 38104-3203
Phone: (901) 527-0841 / Fax: (901) 528-1172

TEXAS

Perishable Food Program
Capital Area Food Bank of Texas
P.O. Box 18311
Austin, TX 78760
Phone: (512) 448-2111 / Fax: (512) 448-2524

The Dallas Hunger Link
North Texas Food Bank
4306 Shilling Way
Dallas, TX 75237
Phone: (214) 330-1396 / Fax: (214) 331-4104

Rescue Mission of El Paso
1949 West Paisano
El Paso, TX 79922
Phone: (915) 532-2575 / Fax: (915) 532-2762

End Hunger Food Loop
End Hunger Network—Houston
1770 St. James, Suite 204
Houston, TX 70056
Phone: (713) 963-0099 / Fax: (713) 963-0199

Houston Food Bank
3811 Eastex Freeway
Houston, TX 77026
Phone: (713) 223-3700 / Fax: (713) 223-1424

Laredo Regional Food Bank, Inc.
P.O. Box 6487
Laredo, TX 78042
Phone: (210) 723-3725

Second Helpings
    South Plains Food Bank
    4612 Locust
    Lubbock, TX 79404
    Phone: (806) 763-3003 / Fax: (806) 741-0850

Second Servings
    San Antonio Food Bank
    4311 Director Drive
    San Antonio, TX 78219
    Phone: (210) 337-3663 / Fax: (210) 337-2646

One Point of Light
    c/o The Volunteer Center
    3000 Texas Boulevard
    Texarkana, TX 75503
    Phone: (903) 793-4903

UTAH

Give S.O.M.E.
    Utah Food Bank
    212 West 1300 Street
    Salt Lake City, UT 84115
    Phone: (801) 486-2136 / Fax: (801) 486-2140

VIRGINIA

Southwestern Virginia Second Harvest Food Bank
    1111 Shenandoah Avenue, N.W.
    P.O. Box 2868
    Roanoke, VA 24001-2868
    Phone: (703) 342-3011 / Fax: (703) 342-0056

Virginia's Table—Peninsula
    Foodbank of the Virginia Peninsula
    9912 Hosier Street
    Newport News, VA 23601
    Phone: (804) 596-7188 / Fax: (804) 595-2507

Virginia's Table
  Central Virginia Food Bank
  4444 Sarellen Road
  Richmond, VA 23231
  Phone: (804) 226-9013 / Fax: (804) 226-9034

Virginia's Table
  Foodbank of Southeastern Virginia
  2308 Granby Street
  Norfolk, VA 23517
  Phone: (804) 624-1333 / Fax: (804) 627-8588

WASHINGTON

Seattle's Table
  Food Lifeline
  15230 15 Avenue, N.E.
  Seattle, WA 98155
  Phone: (206) 545-6567 / Fax: (206) 545-6616

WISCONSIN

Paul's Pantry
  St. Vincent De Paul
  1529 Webster Street
  Green Bay, WI 54302
  Phone: (414) 435-4040

CANADA

Second Harvest Food Support Committee
  444 Yonge Street
  Toronto, Ontario M5B 2H4
  Canada
  Phone: (416) 408-2594 / Fax: (416) 408-2598

ASSOCIATE MEMBERS

The Professional Convention Management Association
  100 Vestavia Office Park, #220
  Birmingham, AL 35216
  Phone: (205) 823-7262 / Fax: (205) 822-3891

Food Bank of Iowa
  30 Northeast 48 Place
  Des Moines, IA 50313
  Phone: (515) 244-6555 / Fax: (515) 244-6556

Dare to Care, Inc.
  P.O. Box 35458
  Louisville, KY 40232
  Phone: (502) 966-3821 / Fax: (502) 966-3827

Project M.A.N.A.
  P.O. Box 3980
  Incline Village, NV 89450
  Phone: (702) 831-3220

Food Donation Connection
  1920 Light Tower Circle
  Hixson, TN 37343
  Phone: (615) 842-1446 / Fax: (615) 842-0973

Subject Index

Menu and Recipe Index